the credit crunch cookbook

the
credit crunch
cookbook

delicious recipes and clever ideas
for cooking on a budget

hamlyn

Essex County Council Libraries

An Hachette Livre UK Company
www.hachettelivre.co.uk

First published in Great Britain in 2009 by Hamlyn,
a division of Octopus Publishing Group Ltd
2–4 Heron Quays, London E14 4JP
www.octopusbooks.co.uk

ISBN 978-0-600-61977-2

A CIP catalogue record for this book is available from the British Library

Printed and bound in China

10 9 8 7 6 5 4 3 2 1

While all reasonable care has been taken during the preparation of this edition, neither the publishers, editors, nor the authors can accept responsibility for any consequences arising from the use of this information.

Standard level spoon measurements are used in all recipes.
1 tablespoon = one 15 ml spoon
1 teaspoon = one 5 ml spoon

Both imperial and metric measurements have been given in all recipes. Use one set of measurements only and not a mixture of both.

Eggs should be medium unless otherwise stated. The Department of Health advises that eggs should not be consumed raw. This book contains dishes made with raw or lightly cooked eggs. It is prudent for more vulnerable people such as pregnant and nursing mothers, invalids, the elderly, babies and young children to avoid uncooked or lightly cooked dishes made with eggs. Once prepared these dishes should be kept refrigerated and used promptly.

This book includes dishes made with nuts and nut derivatives. It is advisable for those with known allergic reactions to nuts and nut derivatives and those who may be potentially vulnerable to these allergies, such as pregnant and nursing mothers, invalids, the elderly, babies and children, to avoid dishes made with nuts and nut oils. It is also prudent to check the labels of pre-prepared ingredients for the possible inclusion of nut derivatives.

Milk should be full fat unless otherwise stated.

Fresh herbs should be used unless otherwise stated. If unavailable, use dried herbs as an alternative but halve the quantities stated.

Ovens should be preheated to the specific temperature – if using a fan-assisted oven, follow manufacturer's instructions for adjusting the time and the temperature. Grills should also be preheated.

contents

introduction

We live in an uncertain world, but two things we can be sure about are that food is going to become an ever-more precious resource and that even those of us who aren't on a tight budget need to treat food with more respect. The days of extravagant buying, inefficient storage and thoughtless waste need to be put behind us as we face the fact that food cannot be taken for granted: it will get scarcer and it will get more expensive.

So, if your bin is frequently full of discarded leftovers, rotten fruit and veg, meat that is past its use-by date and cheese and yogurt that contain more mould than the manufacturer intended ... take heart, because this book will show you how to make the most of two scarce resources: your money and your food. With an information-packed combination of recipes, stand-alone features on many aspects of economical cooking and advice on various foodstuffs, plus themed menus for when you want that restaurant experience at home, this book is the only guide you will need for living frugally but without sacrificing your enjoyment of food, helping you to cook with care, making the most of the ingredients you have. It won't advise you to turn your lawn into a vegetable patch, recycle the children's pizza crusts, brew your own alcohol or knit your own muesli, but it will encourage you to be clever, to be economical and to control what you buy and what you cook.

We start with Waste Not, Want Not, which is packed with tips on how to avoid waste. It really is all down to putting a bit of thought into the way we treat food. If it cost a lot more than it currently does, and if it weren't so freely available, day and night, we'd probably treat it with much more respect. So, be clever, be canny: don't just roast a chicken and bin what you don't eat: cook a larger one than usual, to maximize energy costs, use some of the remaining meat in a pasta dish the next day, use the smaller scraps, some of the leftover veg and some of the stock made from the carcase for a risotto the following day, and then use any remaining stock and veg in a soup. Four meals for the price of one – that's better than any BOGOF offer!

Be prepared to put a little more effort into your shopping: visit markets and wholefood shops, rather than buying everything from a supermarket, which isn't always the cheapest option we're led to believe it is. Buy seasonally, too, taking advantage of the lower prices of food in season and also experimenting with foods you haven't tried before. Most importantly, plan your shopping like a military campaign: decide on your menu for the week; write a firm and comprehensive list of what you need (taking into account the use of leftovers); stick to this list, ignoring the tempting 'offers' that try to lead you astray; and then cook the meals the list was written for. You will have the right ingredients in the right quantities; you won't have spent any money unnecessarily and you won't waste any food.

Learn to look afresh at the foods we use – eggs, dairy produce, bread, potatoes, pasta, rice, beans and pulses, fish and seafood, poultry, meat, vegetables and fruit – and learn valuable tips on their nutritional benefits and their versatility, and on how to store and use them, including any leftovers. Spare eggs approaching their use-by date? You could just bin them, or you could scramble them, make them into pancakes, use them for egg-fried rice or in huevos rancheros, or separate them and make meringues or a soufflé with the whites and hollandaise sauce or chocolate mousse with the yolks. Bread that is past its best? Whizz it into breadcrumbs or a bread crumble mix to freeze, or make an old-fashioned bread and butter pudding – pure comfort food, and extremely cheap. Essentially, there is always something useful you can do with food, and only rarely (usually when it's pretty well walking out of the refrigerator on its own legs) is the bin the only option.

The three chapters – Budget Basics, Impress for Less and Dine In – are full of tasty and inventive recipes, many creating classic favourites using simple, inexpensive ingredients; some maximizing storecupboard ingredients; others being composed almost entirely of leftovers; and yet more based on economical ingredients cooked with thought and flair to create appetizing dishes.

Budget Basics does just what is says on the tin – it provides basic, tasty, everyday meals for the family, day in, day out, which is just what you need. We might aspire to cooking lobster thermidor and rack of lamb every day for our nearest and dearest, but in the real world, where we have to count the pennies, we need reliable, satisfying staples such as soups, stews and crumbles. From popular classics, such as Minestrone Soup, to hearty and satisfying dishes with a difference, such as Pumpkin and Root Vegetable Stew, and old favourites with a twist, such as Cinnamon Doughnuts, here are sufficient recipes to keep your family happy and well fed. Try dishes using economical ingredients, such as Sausage and Bean Casserole, dishes based largely on leftovers, such as Linguine with Shredded Ham and Egg, and dishes made economical by involving a spot of hedgerow foraging first, such as Blackberry Muffin Slice. (And don't even think about buying blackberries in a plastic container from a supermarket: they're provided free, by nature, on a prickly bush somewhere near your home!)

Impress for Less contains recipes for high days and holidays, or at least for those days when you want something a bit different. It's all too easy to think that you can't entertain friends or treat the family to something special if you're watching the pennies, but the recipes here will prove you wrong. Choose from the tempting array of starters, side dishes, main courses and desserts to create menus that will wow friends and family alike. And you won't believe how easy it is to transform an ordinary meal into something quite special. Try replacing boring old boiled potatoes and carrots with scalloped potatoes and honey carrots – at minimal extra cost – and an everyday meal instantly becomes something more impressive. And if the main course or dessert is already

using the oven, there's no extra energy cost either. Fancy treating
yourself to a nice piece of fish, but conscious that it can be a bit pricey?
Just team it up with cheap-as-chips lentils and the dish suddenly
becomes much more economical, and extra nutritious. As for desserts:
rice pudding is a good old-fashioned choice, and cheap too, but that's
for everyday fare: instead, ring the changes at little extra cost by making
it into a chocolate risotto and just watch everyone's face brighten!

Dine In is the chapter you need when you really want to treat yourself
but just can't justify the cost of going out. Even a takeaway can be
prohibitively expensive, especially if there are quite a few mouths to
feed, so it's time to cook it yourself. The thought of making a whole
themed meal might be daunting, but all the recipes here are easy to
follow, and if you rope in the whole family, you'll find it's ready before
you know it. You'll also have fun working together as a team (as long as
everyone is clear as to who is chef and who are the sous chefs!). Fancy
some spicy Thai fishcakes? Just bung all the ingredients in a food
processor and whizz them up, shape into cakes and fry. What could be
easier, or more delicious? Follow that with Green Chicken Curry – with
its wonderful, comforting combination of green curry paste and coconut
milk – and crunchy, tasty Pad Thai, with its great mixture of flavours and
textures. Finish the meal off with Banana Fritters (what could be
cheaper?) and you've had a fantastic meal for probably less than the
cost of one main course in a restaurant. Once you've got the bug, you
could try Mexican, Chinese, Indian and Italian meals too. The benefits?
You get great, healthy food, freshly prepared with no sneaky additives,
cooked when you want it and with money to spare for a bottle of wine.
The downside? The profits of your favourite local takeaway or
restaurant are down a little. Not a difficult choice!

It isn't rocket science to make the most of what our farmers grow and
rear and what our fishermen catch; nor is it a challenging concept to
shop wisely and cook carefully, wasting as little as possible. It's just
common sense. And very tasty it is, too!

waste not,

want not

being *careful*

It is estimated that one-third of all the food we buy ends up in the bin. While this might seem like an extraordinary amount, if you take a minute to think about it you will probably agree that you throw out an awful lot of food. In our fast-paced, consumer-led society, we have perhaps become too accustomed to the wide availability and abundance of ingredients with which many countries are blessed. However, since no one wants to waste money, and since food is gradually becoming a scarcer resource, it is definitely time to shop more wisely and waste less food. So many of the basic foodstuffs we use, such as eggs, cheese, bread and pasta, are much more versatile than you might think, and leftovers can be reused in a wide variety of dishes rather than being consigned to a landfill site. Being careful with what we buy is, quite simply, a win-win situation: we don't waste money and we don't waste food.

having too much choice

We are often a little too hasty when it comes to purging the refrigerator and vegetable rack of those odds and ends that our grannies or mothers would have made into soups and stews. In fact, the frugal habits that were a legacy of wartime rationing have been all but eradicated in recent years, and are more likely to be scorned than emulated in these days of apparent plenty. But just look at some of the ideas in this chapter, and you'll think again. Whether it's making some tasty stock from a chicken carcase, freezing odds and ends of cheese, using up some egg whites in a delicious meringue or making a creamy custard with some milk you didn't need, you'll find all sorts of ways to make the most of what you buy.

As consumers, we have never had it so good. Many supermarkets are now open 24 hours a day, so we can shop whenever we like. In addition, online shopping means that we don't even need to leave the house to do the weekly food shop, as we can now choose, order, arrange delivery and pay for our groceries online.

We can also buy foods from all over the world, which means that if we want strawberries all year round, we can have them – though at a cost to our pocket and the environment. As we learn to reassess our spending patterns and wasteful habits, so our awareness of environmental issues continues to grow. Adjusting your food buying and consuming habits will therefore help both your wallet and the environment.

avoiding false bargains

When we shop, we are bombarded with special offers, discount savings and bulk-buy deals. These actively encourage us to buy more than we really need in order to make apparent savings, although in reality many of these special offers are a false economy. We get caught up in the frenzy of bagging a bargain and buy far more than we are realistically going to be able to consume. While there's nothing more satisfying than looking at a lovely full refrigerator after you have unpacked all your shopping, there's nothing more wasteful than having to throw out perfectly good food because the use-by date has expired.

Just because you CAN get two bags of carrots for the price of one doesn't mean that you are suddenly going to want to eat twice as many carrots as usual. Chances are, the second bag will end up on the compost heap or, worse still, in the bin. However, if you are clever, you can use these deals to your advantage: buy the carrots and get the free bag, then make batches of Carrot and Lentil Soup (see page 63) to pop in the freezer.

visiting markets

When we do our weekly shop we are used to seeing uniform rows and boxes of perfectly shaped fruit and vegetables. This is due to the stringent regulations that are placed on producers to supply produce that fits strict standards. If a carrot is too knobbly or a cucumber is not straight enough, it simply won't make the grade and is quite likely to be discarded. However, in recent years there has been a bit of a backlash, with consumers beginning to appreciate that fruit and vegetables do not have to look identical or perfect to taste good. Thankfully, the increased popularity of farmers' markets has done a lot for the street cred of humble fruit and veg. People have discovered that shopping at these markets enables them to save money as well as buying locally produced fresh food.

In order to make the most of your local farmers' market, you should try to plan recipes to fit in with seasonal produce. If there is a particular fruit or vegetable that has a relatively short season – such as asparagus or raspberries – buy more than you need, then freeze some either as it is or in a made dish to be enjoyed later.

taking control

With just a few changes to your shopping and eating habits and a little bit of planning, you could be saving pounds on your weekly food bill. This chapter will give you plenty of ideas on how to make the most of all the food you buy, with ideas for using up leftovers, as well as making the most of products with a limited shelf life.

think before you throw

*Canny consumer's
shopping list*

Kitchen foil

Clingfilm

Freezer bags (self-seal
  are best)

Freezer bag pen or stickers

Freezerproof boxes
  (or re-use ice cream and
  other food cartons)

Preserving jars (for jams,
  chutneys and sauces)

The next time you are about to throw out a few lonely vegetables in the bottom of the refrigerator or the last bit of chicken left over from the Sunday roast, stop first and think if there is any way you can use them up. We often banish food to the bin needlessly. It might be that we are making space for shopping, clearing out the refrigerator, or simply too busy to invent a dish that will make use of the odds and ends or leftovers from previous meals.

common culprits

There are certain foods that most people tend to consign to the bin without the slightest feeling of guilt. Whilst a bag of sprouting potatoes or a bunch of overripe bananas might get discarded with a little shame, some foodstuffs are simply seen as waste and are tossed aside with no thought as to how they might be incorporated into a meal. Not only does this create unnecessary waste but it also means that you are missing out on some great flavours by ignoring these unloved ingredients.

celery tops These tasty, nutritious parts of celery are usually sliced off and pushed to one side. If you don't want to add them to a salad, then use them in stir-fries or to add flavour to soups.

chicken carcase This should never be thrown away without first being simmered in a large pot with some water, onion, carrot and celery. After it has bubbled for a couple of hours on the hob, you will be rewarded with your own delicious stock, which can be used as a base for soups or added to risottos and stews.

stalks Whether it's mushrooms, broccoli or herbs, we seem to have an aversion to stalks. In many instances, the stalks actually contain a higher concentration of the vitamins and flavour than the bits we do eat, and there is absolutely no reason to discard them. Instead, chop them up and use them in risottos, stews, stir-fries or soups.

shopping savvy

If the food isn't there, it can't be thrown out, which means that sensible shopping habits are actually the best way to avoid food wastage. If you plan your weekly meals and shop accordingly, then you really shouldn't need to throw out any food, as it will all be accounted for throughout the week.

Most people know in advance if there are any nights when they won't be eating at home, or any days when they will be away. So, it should be relatively easy to plan the week's meals in advance, write a comprehensive shopping list and stick to it rigidly once you arrive at the supermarket. Remember to include extras such as breakfast items and any particular snacks you like. You might be trying to save money, but there is no point being overly frugal in the supermarket and then buying snacks and drinks when you are out and about.

use it or lose it

Once you get your shopping home, it is important to keep to your recipe plan or, if you are going to change anything, make sure that the food for the planned meal can be otherwise used. You should check your refrigerator every few days for items that are close to their 'use-by' date. If there is anything that has to be eaten or thrown out, you can try to adjust the menu plan slightly to accommodate it. Likewise, check the freezer every so often: it is easy for bags and boxes to get pushed to the back and forgotten. You don't want to go to the effort of saving your leftovers only to have to discard them months later because they are too old to use.

If you are going to get into the habit of using up every last scrap of food in the refrigerator and cupboards, then you need to be prepared. There really isn't that much to it, but there are some essential items that you should keep in the kitchen (see page 14).

Tips for cost-effective food shopping

Write a weekly menu plan with a list of the ingredients you will need.

•

Take a list when you go shopping and don't be tempted to buy any extras.

•

Take a calculator and cash (no cards) so you can't spend over your budget.

•

Never shop on an empty stomach.

•

Don't be swayed by special offers, unless it is food you know you will use.

•

Shop towards the end of the day for marked-down items.

•

Buy less-popular cuts of meat and varieties of fish — just as tasty but a lot cheaper.

eggs

Eggs are one of those foodstuffs that tend to appear on most people's shopping lists. They are seen as a storecupboard staple and, along with bread and milk, are probably one of the most common items that we regularly buy. However, as they tend to have a relatively long shelf life, they often get pushed to the back of the refrigerator as new food arrives. There they hide, forgotten and unused, until it is too late and they have to be thrown away.

deliciously versatile

The humble egg has so many culinary uses that it seems crazy that we end up throwing so many of them away. Not only can they be eaten on their own in a number of different ways but they are also indispensable when it comes to baking. As they are so versatile, there really isn't any excuse for thinking that you just don't feel like eating eggs for dinner.

If you have eggs that need using up, there are endless options for deliciously quick and nutritious meals. Whether it is just the one lonely egg left in the box, or half a dozen that have been overlooked, there are so many ways to eat eggs that it doesn't matter what the occasion is – there will always be something that fits the bill.

storage

The debate rages on as to where we should store eggs. Although supermarkets do not generally keep eggs in a chiller cabinet, eggs do tend to last longer if they are kept at a regulated temperature. Domestic kitchens have fluctuating temperatures, so it is probably best to store them in the refrigerator once you get them home. Always follow the use-by date that is stamped on your eggs. It is usually a fairly generous few weeks, although obviously the quality will gradually deteriorate over this time and some dishes work best with the eggs being as fresh as possible.

using up yolks and whites

While whole eggs can be used up for a quick snack or an easy meal, it isn't quite so straightforward to come up with ideas for using up just the yolks or whites. It is common to have a number of these left over after baking, and although you might put them in the refrigerator with the intention of using them for something else, all too often they sit there day after day until they are only good for the bin. Egg yolks (left intact) and whites tend to last for about 2–3 days in the refrigerator, after they have been separated, so you will need to come up with some ideas to use them within this time. Here are a few quick ideas to make the most of the other half of the egg.

Whites	Yolks
Freeze in small batches	Freeze individual yolks in ice-cube tray holes
Meringue	Hollandaise sauce
Soufflé	Aïoli
Egg-white omelette	Chocolate mousse
Scrambled egg whites	Crême patissière

Ten ways to put eggs on the menu

1 Scrambled egg on toasted bagel
2 Pancakes
3 French toast
4 Egg-fried rice
5 Omelette
6 Fried-egg sandwich
7 Eggs Benedict
8 Salade Niçoise
9 Huevos rancheros
10 Scotch egg

cointreau
chocolate pots
with orange salad

serves 4

300 ml (½ pint) single cream

200 g (7 oz) good-quality milk
   chocolate, broken into small pieces

2 egg yolks

2 tablespoons Cointreau

finely grated rind of 2 oranges

25 g (1 oz) slightly salted butter

for the orange salad

50 g (2 oz) caster sugar

50 ml (2 fl oz) water

2 oranges

lemon juice, to taste

1 Pour the cream into a saucepan and allow to warm through, but do not let it boil. Remove the pan from the heat and add the chocolate, stirring well until it has all melted. Beat in the egg yolks, Cointreau and orange rind, then stir in the butter and leave it to melt.

2 Line 4 ramekins or shallow dishes with clingflim. Pour the chocolate mixture into the ramekins and leave to set in the refrigerator for a couple of hours or overnight.

3 To make the orange salad, heat the sugar and water in a small pan, stirring until the sugar dissolves. Bring to the boil, then simmer for 1 minute before removing the pan from the heat and leaving to cool.

4 Finely grate the orange rind and add that to the pan with a squeeze of lemon juice to balance the sweetness. Remove and discard the remaining rind and pith, then slice the oranges and add them to the salad. Leave to one side until ready to serve.

5 Remove the chocolate pots from the refrigerator and turn out on to a plate 20 minutes before serving. Serve with the orange salad.

1 Put the strawberries and 1 tablespoon of the sugar in a saucepan and cook over a low heat until the strawberries become soft and start to release some of their liquid. Tip them into a food processor or liquidizer and blend until smooth, then pass the purée through a fine sieve to remove the seeds. Return the pan to the boil, then simmer for about 5 minutes until the purée is reduced to a thick and jammy consistency. Set aside to cool completely.

2 Whisk the egg whites until they form stiff peaks. Place the remaining sugar and 50 ml (2 fl oz) of the water in a small saucepan and bring to the boil, then remove from the heat. Gradually pour the hot sugar syrup into the egg whites, beating all the time. Continue beating the egg whites until cold. Set aside.

3 Soak the gelatine in a bowl of cold water. Whip the cream until it forms fairly firm peaks.

4 Bring the remaining water to the boil in a small pan, then remove the pan from the heat. Squeeze out the excess water from the gelatine and stir it into the hot water until it has dissolved, then pass the gelatine mixture through a sieve into the purée. Fold the cream and purée into the egg whites. Pour the mixture into individual glasses and leave to set. Serve with fresh strawberries.

serves 4

200 g (7 oz) strawberries (or other berries), cut in half, plus extra to serve

65 g (2½ oz) caster sugar

2 egg whites

65 ml (2½ fl oz) water

1½ sheets of leaf gelatine

150 ml (5 fl oz) whipping cream

strawberry *parfait*

hazelnut *meringue* roulade

serves 6—8

1 Line a 33 x 23 cm (13 x 9 inch) Swiss roll tin with nonstick baking paper.

2 Put the egg whites in a large mixing bowl and whisk until stiff but not dry using an electric hand-held mixer on high speed. Gradually add the sugar a tablespoon at a time, then continue whisking on high speed until the meringue is thick and glossy. Fold in the hazelnuts and spread the mixture over the base of the prepared tin.

3 Bake in a preheated oven, 180°C (350°F), Gas Mark 4, for 8–10 minutes until lightly golden, then turn the heat down to 160°C (325°F), Gas Mark 3, and bake for a further 15 minutes until firm to the touch.

4 Remove the meringue from the oven and turn it out on to a piece of nonstick baking paper. Peel the lining paper from the base and leave to cool.

5 Whip the cream until it forms soft peaks and spread it evenly over the cooled meringue. Scatter the raspberries over the cream and roll the meringue up into a roulade from a short end, using the baking paper to help. Dust with icing sugar and serve in thick slices.

5 egg whites

250 g (8 oz) caster sugar

100 g (3½ oz) chopped roasted hazelnuts

200 ml (7 fl oz) double cream

150 g (5 oz) raspberries

2 tablespoons icing sugar, sifted

goats' *cheese* and *bacon tart*

serves 4

for the pastry

300 g (10 oz) plain flour, plus extra for dusting

125 g (4 oz) chilled butter, diced

1 egg, plus 1 egg yolk

for the filling

2 tablespoons olive oil

8–10 streaky bacon rashers, roughly chopped

200 g (7 oz) goats' cheese, crumbled

2 eggs

100 ml (3½ fl oz) double cream

100 ml (3½ fl oz) milk

salt and pepper

1 To make the pastry, sift the flour into a large mixing bowl, add the butter and rub in with the fingertips until the mixture resembles fine breadcrumbs. Gradually add the egg and yolk until the ingredients bind together, adding a drop of water if necessary. On a lightly floured surface, knead the dough briefly until smooth, then wrap in clingfilm and place in the refrigerator for 30 minutes.

2 Roll out the pastry on a lightly floured surface and use to line a 23 cm (9 inch) flan tin. Place in the refrigerator for 30 minutes.

3 Line the pastry case with foil and baking beans and cook in a preheated oven, 200°C (400°F), Gas Mark 6, for 10–12 minutes until lightly golden. Remove the foil and beans and bake for a further 6–8 minutes to dry out the base of the pastry case. Remove from the oven once more and set aside.

4 Heat the olive oil in a frying pan, add the bacon and fry until crispy, then remove from the pan using a slotted spoon and drain on kitchen paper. Spread the bacon and goats' cheese over the pastry case.

5 Put the eggs, cream and milk in a bowl, beat well and season with salt and pepper. Pour the mixture into the tart case and place in the oven for 20–25 minutes until the filling is set. Serve hot or cold.

dairy products

Dairy items such as milk, cheese and yogurts take up a lot of space in most refrigerators. Different dairy products have very differing shelf lives, so it is important to keep a close eye on when individual items are approaching their 'use-by' dates.

the delights of dairy

You probably don't realize quite how many different dairy products you consume on a daily basis. If you enjoy a cup of tea first thing in the morning, then milk is the one that immediately springs to mind. However, there are also butter, yogurt, cream, cheese, sauces and other foods containing dairy, as well as the endless variations that occur within each of these categories. In order to make the most of your dairy goods, you need to ensure that they are stored correctly. Keeping foods at the right temperature can add to their shelf life and ensure maximum flavour. The following table gives refrigerator and freezer storage times, though these are only approximates; always refer to 'use-by' dates.

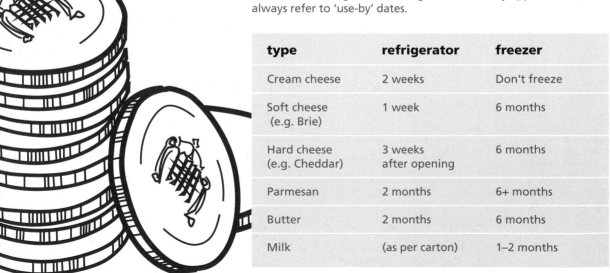

type	refrigerator	freezer
Cream cheese	2 weeks	Don't freeze
Soft cheese (e.g. Brie)	1 week	6 months
Hard cheese (e.g. Cheddar)	3 weeks after opening	6 months
Parmesan	2 months	6+ months
Butter	2 months	6 months
Milk	(as per carton)	1–2 months

look at the labels

As with all foods that have a very specific timeframe in terms of being consumed, you need to be extremely vigilant with dairy products. It goes without saying that you should check the refrigerator regularly. Rotating items so that those with the closest use-by dates are at the front will help you to ensure everything is used up.

You should also be aware of what the label is actually telling you. There is a difference between the terms 'best before' and 'use by'. 'Best before' is more a statement of advice and it indicates that the food will have passed its peak quality after this date. It doesn't, however, mean that it is unsafe to eat, and so you still have a little leeway in terms of consuming the food. On the other hand, a 'use-by' date should be taken as the final date by which the food needs to be consumed. This may be because the food will go off quickly afterwards and there could be a risk of illness if it is eaten after this date. There are a few easy steps you can take to ensure that you get the most out of your dairy items and that they don't go off before their time.

Making the most of dairy products

Check that dairy products feel cold in the shop before you put them in your trolley. Milk should be well chilled and ice cream firm.

•

If you are visiting different shops, buy your milk at the last stop to minimize the amount of time it is out of the refrigerator.

•

Put all dairy products in the refrigerator as soon as you get them back home.

•

Try not to leave milk out of the refrigerator. It is easy to keep it out during breakfast or between tea breaks, but it doesn't take very long for the temperature to rise sufficiently for it to start going sour.

•

Check the storage instructions on packaging. Many items have a long shelf life but need to be used quickly once opened.

•

Try not to store dairy products in the door of the refrigerator. The temperature increases every time you open the refrigerator and this can reduce their shelf life.

•

Keep cheese well wrapped and in a separate container in the refrigerator. Check the cheese regularly for mould and keep the container clean and dry.

Use it tonight

Béchamel sauce
Homemade custard
Ice cream
Corn chowder
Milkshake
Rice pudding
Paneer

Quick cheesy ideas

Macaroni cheese is a
classic supper dish and
a great way to use up
both cheese and milk.

•

Make a cheese sauce to
serve with meat.

•

Cheese on toast can be
transformed by adding
slices of tomato.

•

Grated cheese is the
perfect filling for
baked potatoes.

•

Cream cheese can be
mixed with pesto and
chopped sun-dried
tomatoes to make a
delicious pasta sauce.

milk

Most of us consume a fair quantity of milk, whether in hot drinks, on cereal or straight from the refrigerator. It would therefore seem somewhat crazy to suggest that there might ever be a glut of milk that needed using up. However, it is easy to overestimate the amount you buy and it is good to have a few quick ideas up your sleeve if you double up on milk purchases. Another occasion when milk often goes to waste is just before leaving on holiday (or just after, if you forget to clear the refrigerator). Instead of leaving it until the last minute to throw out anything that won't last, with just a little forward planning you could ensure that nothing goes to waste.

cheese

Cheese comes in so many different varieties that it is difficult to suggest any hard and fast rules for using up leftovers. Some hard cheeses, such as Parmesan, can live happily in the refrigerator for a few months, while soft cheeses such as Brie might last only a week or so. As a general rule, the harder the cheese the longer it will last, but you should always check the packaging to ensure you consume it all by the 'use-by' date.

Many cheeses can actually be frozen, as long as they are very carefully wrapped. Some whole soft cheeses will freeze well, while Cheddar and Parmesan could be grated first, giving you a ready supply of grated cheese to add to dishes such as lasagne. (See page 22 for freezing guides.)

yogurt

Yogurt is basically fermented milk, which doesn't make it sound very appealing. However, its thick, creamy texture certainly makes it a popular addition to the shopping trolley. There are whole aisles dedicated to yogurt in supermarkets and it is one of those items that is often bought in abundance, generally because it is on special offer and probably because you are often so overwhelmed with the choices on offer. You may well love it but perhaps not quite enough to get through three pots a day, and those use-by dates can creep up on you unawares. Luckily, there are plenty of interesting ways to incorporate yogurt into meals and snacks.

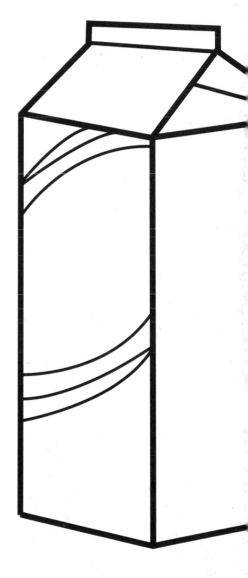

Using up yogurt

Make a breakfast smoothie with any flavoured yogurt. Thin the mixture by adding some milk and add chopped fruit such as strawberries and bananas.

•

Yogurt makes a lovely sauce for fruit salad. Just toss a selection of chopped fruit in a little fruit juice, then stir in spoonfuls of yogurt. This could be flavoured yogurt, or natural yogurt with a spoon of honey to add sweetness.

•

Try replacing milk with yogurt on your muesli — or have a little of both.

•

Kids love anything that is sweet and frozen, so make your own desserts by freezing yogurt in small containers.

•

Natural yogurt makes a great base for a curry sauce.

•

Try something different on your barbecue or under the grill by marinating chicken or lamb in a mixture of yogurt and spices before cooking.

bread

Whether it's rice, pasta or potatoes, every country has its favourite carbohydrate fix. In Britain, this tends to be bread, and we devour it all, from a sliced white loaf for sandwiches to a warm naan accompanying a curry. There is something wonderfully comforting about this staple food: perhaps it is those childhood memories of hot buttered toast. So, it seems a real shame that so much of it is consigned to the bin.

storing bread

Bread can be a little temperamental when it comes to staying fresh. If conditions are too warm, mould will quickly develop as the bread begins to sweat. Therefore, although it is a good idea to store your bread in a breadbin, it shouldn't be wrapped too tightly. Most types of bread freeze well, but before freezing you will need to wrap your bread up securely to stop moisture and air creeping in. Defrosted frozen bread doesn't taste as good as fresh but it is great for an emergency, and if you toast it you probably won't taste the difference.

Baguettes and crusty rolls tend to harden up if they don't get eaten quite soon after you've bought them. As long as they aren't completely solid, they can easily be brought back to life by putting them in a warm oven for a few minutes. If they still seem hard, cut them into slices and top with tomatoes and basil for an instant bruschetta snack.

Use your loaf

Make a week's worth of sandwiches and then freeze them in individual servings. Move a pack to the refrigerator each evening to defrost and add salad the next morning before you set off. That way you don't need to worry about bread going off by the end of the week.

•

When you buy a loaf of bread, split it in half and put one half in the freezer. That way you won't end up throwing it away after a few days if it hasn't all been eaten.

•

Make your own breadcrumbs with those stale ends of bread that always get thrown in the bin. Just tear into pieces, pop into a food processor or liquidizer and whizz into crumbs. You can then freeze them and use as and when required.

•

If any fussy members of your family refuse to eat their crusts, this is another great source of breadcrumbs. Save the crusts for a couple of days and you should have enough for a generous bag.

•

If your bread is looking a little bit worse for wear, you can soften it up by running it very briefly under the cold tap. Remove any excess water and place it in a hot oven for a few minutes to revive it.

bake your own

How about cutting down on wastage and saving money at the same time? The perfect way to do this is by making your own bread. You can bake the type of bread you like to eat and also make smaller loaves so they won't have time to go stale. You don't even need to invest in a bread maker: it is entirely possible to make delicious homemade bread without having to buy any special equipment. However, if you catch the bread-baking bug, you might decide that it is worth investing in a breadmaker – and you will soon recoup your money. Once you get the hang of it, bread is very quick and easy to prepare. The only aspects of bread-making that take any length of time are proving and cooking, and you can sit down and put your feet up during both of those processes.

There's something almost magical about making dough and then seeing it practically grow before your eyes. And then, of course, there is the irresistible smell of freshly baked bread and the fact that you can eat it while it's still warm. You are also in complete control of what goes into your bread: you can choose your own flour, add extra ingredients such as nuts and seeds, and enjoy freshly baked bread every day.

Use it tonight

Breadcrumbs

Bread crumble mix

Croûtons

Bread soup

French toast

Bread and butter pudding

Topping for fish
(breadcrumbs and grated
Parmesan cheese)

Tips for making bread

Make a number of smaller loaves rather than a couple of large ones. That way you can keep out what you need and freeze the remainder.

•

Dough should be left to rise in a place that is warm but not hot.

•

Always cook bread in the centre of the oven so the hot air can move around and cook it evenly.

•

Make a large batch of pizza dough and then cut it into individual portions and freeze the dough that you aren't using. Next time you want to make a pizza, just defrost the dough.

•

Leave bread to cool before you cut it or transfer it to the freezer.

potatoes

Ten fillings for baked potatoes

Tuna, kidney beans and
  red onion

Cream cheese and chives

Chilli topped with sour
  cream

Prawns and mayonnaise

Feta cheese, chickpeas
  and cucumber

Ratatouille

Leftover curry

Chopped cooked chicken
  and pesto

Chopped smoked salmon,
  cream cheese and dill

Natural yogurt,
  cucumber and mint

Potatoes are almost certainly one of the most versatile vegetables. They are also very nutritious and economical and they keep well, if stored in the correct conditions. As an ingredient, they can be prepared and cooked in so many different ways and they have their place at practically any meal, from breakfast to sides or main dishes.

choosing potatoes

There are literally hundreds of different varieties of potato available. Each type is more suited to a specific cooking method or recipe; and, likewise, when it comes to storage, there are variations too. For most of your everyday dishes, there are really two main types of potato to choose between, depending on what you are cooking. When deciding upon specific varieties, it really comes down to personal taste.

waxy Varieties such as Charlotte hold their shape well when cooked, which makes them a good choice for dishes such as potato salad. Waxy potatoes will slice neatly as they have a dense, creamy texture.

floury These have a lighter texture and a fluffy consistency so they are good for roasting or mashing. Look out for varieties such as Desiree and Maris Piper.

storage and shelf life

If you treat your potatoes properly they will reward you with a long shelf life. The potato is a fantastic basic ingredient that marries well with very many flavours. In fact, its versatility has meant that it is widely used in many cuisines around the world. Here are some tips for keeping potatoes at their prime.

• Buy potatoes that still have soil on them and don't wash them before storing. Avoid buying the pre-washed varieties in plastic bags, as they won't last as long.

• Once home, store potatoes in a paper bag or hesian sack or place on a plastic rack with ventilation holes.
• Store them in a cool, dry place but somewhere not too cold – they must not be exposed to frost.
• Keep them stored away from foods that have strong odours.
• Check them regularly and remove any that have started sprouting.
• New potatoes will be past their best just a few days after purchase. Make sure you use them quickly to make the most of their deliciously creamy flavour. However, older varieties should keep for a month or more, as long as they are stored correctly.

making the most of spuds

Whatever you have planned for a meal, there is usually some way to incorporate potatoes. So, if you notice that those new potatoes aren't looking quite so new any more, don't just ignore them: try one of these simple ideas to use them up.

homemade chips These are easy to prepare and a healthy alternative to deep-fried chips. Peel the potatoes, trim the ends and cut into even-sized pieces. Par-boil for a minute or so, then drain well, pat dry and toss in a little olive oil. Transfer to a baking tray in a hot oven and cook, turning occasionally, until golden and cooked through.

potato soup Peel and chop some potatoes and place in a pan with any other leftover vegetables. Just cover with water and boil until tender. Season well, then purée until smooth.

cheesy mash As the name suggests, this is mash with plenty of grated cheese mixed in at the end. For the best results, always drain your potatoes well, then add a little milk and a knob of butter before mashing.

fish cakes These might sound difficult but they can be prepared in a matter of minutes. Combine a drained can of tuna (or some cooked, flaked fish) with a little beaten egg and a couple of dessertspoonfuls of mashed potato. Season and combine, then shape into patties. Dust with flour, dip in breadcrumbs and either grill or shallow-fry until golden.

potato salad Baby new potatoes work really well in this classic side dish. Boil the potatoes until tender, drain well and leave them to cool slightly. Mix some mayonnaise, olive oil and snipped chives together in a bowl, then add the potatoes and coat in the dressing.

baked potato

Baked potatoes are a cost-effective alternative to a ready-meal as they are the ideal choice for a quick dinner but don't take any longer to cook than a plastic-wrapped meal. For an ultra-speedy supper, rinse and dry a baking potato then prick with a fork and pop it in the microwave. The potato should be cooked by the time you have prepared the filling. Alternatively, you can start cooking in the microwave then finish the potato in a hot oven for a deliciously golden, crispy skin. If you have baking potatoes that need using up, chances are there is something in the cupboard or refrigerator that would make a delicious filling. The panel opposite has a few ideas to inspire you.

champ
potato cakes

1 Heat the mashed potato in the microwave or in a saucepan. Mix in the butter and enough flour to make a pliable, but not too dry, dough, then stir in the spring onions and season with salt and pepper.

2 Turn the potato mixture out on to a floured surface and roll out until about 2.5 cm (1 inch) thick. Using a 5 cm (2 inch) circular pastry cutter, cut out the dough into 8 rounds.

3 Heat a frying pan over a high heat and add 1 tablespoon of the olive oil. Fry half the potato cakes for 2–3 minutes on each side, or until golden brown, then remove and keep warm while you repeat with the remaining oil and potato cakes.

4 Serve the potato cakes with a simple fried egg and some streaky bacon or with a warming winter stew.

serves 4

250 g (8 oz) mashed potato

3 tablespoons melted butter

about 65 g (2½ oz) plain flour, plus extra for dusting

3 spring onions, finely sliced

2 tablespoons olive oil

salt and pepper

serves 4

for the curry paste

2 dried long red chillies, deseeded and chopped

1 tablespoon coriander seeds

1 tablespoon cumin seeds

¼ teaspoon white peppercorns

2 cloves

2 cardamom pods

1 star anise

1.5 cm (¾ inch) piece of cinnamon stick

2 tablespoons vegetable oil

1 onion, finely chopped

2.5 cm (1 inch) piece of fresh root ginger, peeled and chopped

2 garlic cloves

1 lemongrass stalk, finely chopped

1 teaspoon palm sugar or brown sugar

for the curry

2 tablespoons vegetable oil

2 kaffir lime leaves

400 ml (14 fl oz) can coconut milk

3 large waxy potatoes, peeled and cut into 1.5 cm (¾ inch) dice

1 tablespoon fish sauce (nam pla)

50 g (2 oz) salted peanuts

Thai sticky (glutinous) rice, to serve

1 To make the curry paste, dry-fry all the dried spices in a frying pan over a moderate heat for a few minutes until they become fragrant. Grind to a fine powder in a clean coffee or spice grinder or using a mortar and pestle. Set aside.

2 Heat the oil in a frying pan and sauté the onion, ginger, garlic and lemongrass until softened and slightly brown. Scrape the mixture on to a plate and leave to cool slightly, then place the mixture in a food processor or liquidizer with the ground spices and sugar and blend until smooth.

3 To make the curry, heat the oil in a large saucepan, add the curry paste and fry for a minute or so until fragrant. Add the kaffir lime leaves, coconut milk and potatoes and bring to the boil, then cover and simmer until the potatoes are cooked.

4 Remove the lime leaves and stir in the fish sauce. Add a little more sugar if needed. Finally, add the peanuts and serve with Thai sticky rice.

massaman curry

pasta and rice

Rice and pasta are filling and nutritious, as well as being quick and easy to prepare. From simple family suppers to more adventurous dinner party dishes, these two ingredients can always rise to the occasion. However, we are often a little generous when it comes to estimating portion sizes and cook far more than is needed. How many times have you scraped half a pan of unused pasta or rice into the bin at the end of a meal?

measuring up

The easiest way to cut down on pasta and rice wastage is to measure out the amounts of dry or uncooked ingredients accurately. If you have the correct amounts to begin with, you shouldn't need to throw anything away once it is cooked. This also means that you are eating the correct portion size for your meals. This is important, as overestimating food portions can be a contributing factor in weight gain.

	dry weight side dish	**dry weight** main course
Rice	50 g (2 oz)	75 g (3 oz)
Pasta	50–75 g (2–3 oz)	100 g (3½ oz)

While kitchen scales will undoubtedly supply the most accurate measurements, a mug or your hand can be a pretty good measure too. A quarter of an average-sized mug is a pretty good indicator of an adult's main course portion of rice, and you can usually work on the basis that a couple of generous handfuls of uncooked pasta per person should be sufficient. A spaghetti measurer is a cheap, simple device that will help with spaghetti amounts.

Tips for kids' meals

Cook up a big batch of pasta and keep it in an airtight container in the refrigerator. You then have cooked pasta ready to use for the next few days. Stir in a little olive oil once it has drained to stop it sticking.

•

If the kids love spaghetti but find it a bit tricky to eat, snap the strands into smaller lengths before cooking. It is easier to do it when uncooked as you can make them the same size. It should also cut down on waste as the smaller strands make it easier to see how much you need.

•

A few pasta shapes left in the bottom of the bag might not be sufficient for an adult meal but will probably be just right for a child's portion. Alternatively, save the ends of a couple of bags of different pasta shapes and cook them together for a pasta medley.

•

If there isn't even enough for a child's meal in the bottom of the bag, donate any odd pasta shapes to the craft box — they are great for making pictures or necklaces!

Using up leftovers

Ready-made lunch If you have some leftover pasta and sauce, just transfer it to a sealed container and take it into work for lunch the following day. It's quick, easy and cheaper than buying a sandwich.

•

Pasta salad Leftover pasta is great for rustling up a quick salad. Just combine it with some pesto, chopped red pepper and chopped tomatoes and serve with crusty bread.

•

Rice and bean salad Use up cooked rice by adding some kidney beans, chickpeas, sweetcorn and chopped parsley.

•

A bit on the side Simply serve leftover pasta or rice as a side dish for the following day's meal. You can liven it up with some extra ingredients or just keep it plain for an accompaniment to curry or chilli con carne.

•

Pasta bake Combine leftover pasta with a cheese sauce and top with a mixture of grated Parmesan cheese and breadcrumbs. Pop under the grill until golden brown on top.

safe use of leftovers

As with all cooked foods, there are certain rules that need to be adhered to when storing, reheating and eating cooked rice and pasta. Once cooked, allow the food to cool completely. You can do this quickly by draining it in a colander and running some cold water through it. Rice in particular should not be left at room temperature for too long. Transfer the pasta or rice to sealed containers and place in the refrigerator. Rice should ideally be eaten the following day, but cooked pasta should last a couple of days. If you are reheating the rice or pasta, it is important to ensure it is hot throughout. Never reheat it more than once.

beans *and* pulses

So, you opened a can of kidney beans but only used half, or you overestimated the amount of lentils to soak and now have a huge bowl of them left over. These are common dilemmas, but there is no need to throw anything away because beans and pulses can be sneaked into all manner of dishes.

on the pulse

Beans and pulses are nutritious, filling and very economical, and an ideal source of protein for vegetarians. They can be used to bulk out stews and casseroles, add texture and flavour to soups and turn light dishes into more hearty meals. There are so many pulses to choose from and you can generally buy them either dried or canned (pre-cooked and ready to use). Dried pulses need to be soaked in water before use and can take anything from an hour to overnight to soak sufficiently. However, if you plan your meals in advance, this is easy to do. Canned pulses are a great storecupboard staple and, although they will work out to be more expensive than dried, they are great for last-minute additions to recipes.

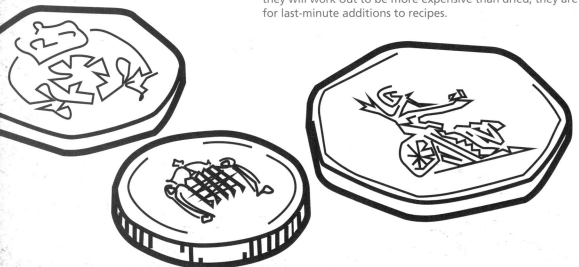

Cooking and storing tips

Store beans and pulses in airtight containers in a cool, dry place.

•

Estimate approximately 50 g (2 oz) of dried pulses per person and bear in mind that once they have been soaked and cooked they will roughly double in weight.

•

Leave them to soak overnight if possible; that way you know they will be ready to cook when you need them.

•

Always rinse away the soaking water thoroughly before cooking.

•

Once cooked, if you are not using them immediately, cool and transfer the pulses quickly to the refrigerator or freezer. You should eat cooked pulses within two days.

•

If freezing, place them in freezer bags and seal tightly. To get rid of as much air as possible, push a straw in at one corner and suck out the excess air.

leftover, not left out

Here are some quick and simple ideas for leftover pulses. They could be dried pulses that you have soaked or the remains of a can of pre-cooked pulses that need using up. These are just some of the many varieties available, but many of these ideas can be transferred to other pulses – this is just a taster to get you started.

kidney beans
- Bean salad with butter beans, chickpeas and chopped herbs
- Mexican-style wraps with avocado, cooked chicken and soured cream
- Roughly mashed with olive oil as a dip or on toast
- Homemade chilli con carne

lentils
- Homemade dhal
- Part of soups or casseroles
- Lentil dip
- Filling for stuffed peppers along with feta cheese

chickpeas
- Homemade hummus
- Falafels
- A curry side dish with chopped tomatoes and spices
- Salad with feta cheese and cherry tomatoes

baked beans
- Sausage and bean casserole
- Mixed with a little chilli powder and served with baked potatoes
- Part of a cooked breakfast
- Combined with grated cheese for a delicious toasted sandwich
- Bean and potato pie
- As a filling with sausages for Yorkshire pudding

fish and *seafood*

There's nothing like a lovely piece of fresh fish for dinner, but, as with all other food, just because it tastes good doesn't mean it will all be eaten. You might have got carried away with a special offer, defrosted more than you need, or maybe the kids turned their noses up at it and just ate the mashed potato. Whatever the reason, don't throw it out!

careful handling

Fish and seafood need to be treated with care when it comes to storing, cooking and reheating. As long as they are kept in the refrigerator and you take note of the use-by date, you have endless options for deliciously quick meals. If you don't know what to buy, your fishmonger will be able to offer advice on varieties and cuts, as well as perhaps recommending the cooking techniques that best suit that particular fish or seafood.

lovely leftovers

Transfer any leftover fish to the refrigerator as soon as possible. You should use it up the following day and, if you need to reheat the fish, you should make sure it is piping hot all the way through. As fish is quite delicate, there is a risk that it will dry out, so a quick burst of high heat is better than prolonged cooking. Try sprinkling a few drops of water over the top before reheating to stop it becoming too dry.

Save more, waste less

If you buy packs of salmon fillets or other fish, separate them into one- or two-portion parcels before freezing. That way, you won't need to defrost the whole pack for one meal.

•

Cut fish fillets or steaks into two or three pieces; each of these can be used as a child's serving. This will cut down on wastage when you defrost.

•

Frozen cooked prawns defrost quickly if you run them under the cold tap. This means you can add just a handful to a dish without needing to defrost and use a whole bag in one meal.

•

If you have fish in the refrigerator that needs using up urgently but you don't want to eat it today, make a fish pie and pop it in the freezer for another occasion.

•

Different varieties of fish go in and out of fashion. Choose less-popular varieties to save money.

•

Shop at a fishmonger's for greater variety. It might prove cheaper to buy whole fish and get them gutted and cleaned than to buy fillets.

•

Stretch your budget by turning one fish fillet into four fish cakes. Mashed potato, herbs and seasoning will add plenty of flavour.

fish for kids

Fish, particularly oily fish, is a great source of omega-3 fatty acids and it can have an important role to play in the diets of growing children. However, persuading kids to eat food that is good for them is often harder than it sounds. Fish is one of those foods that we seem to develop more of a taste for as we get older. While some children will happily tuck into a plate of cod and vegetables, others will simply not even try it. Here are a few easy ways to get the kids to eat fish without a fuss.

pasta sauce If you have any leftover canned tuna, you can add it to a tomato sauce and serve with pasta.

pizza bread Alternatively, cut a ciabatta roll or small baguette in half, top with the sauce and place under the grill for a few minutes. Top with grated cheese, grill for another minute until the cheese has melted and you have delicious pizza bread.

fish fingers Cut white fish fillets into thin strips and top with a mixture of grated cheese and breadcrumbs. Grill until heated through (previously cooked fish) or cooked (raw fish) and the cheese has melted.

fishy potato Add a little flaked salmon to mashed potato: the children probably won't even notice it is there.

Ten ways to use up leftover fish

1   Fish pie
2   Fish cakes
3   Kedgeree
4   Fish stew
5   Topping for baked potatoes
6   Topping for bruschetta
7   Fish soup
8   Sandwich filling (mixed with mayonnaise)
9   Dip (mixed with cream cheese)
10   Added to scrambled eggs

poultry

There is a particular domestic scene that is common in households around the country every Sunday. The chicken is carved and served, lunch is eaten and everyone is fed and happy... then afterwards the carcase is scraped into the bin along with any leftovers. However, it is time to change your habits and make more of this fabulous source of protein.

quality not quantity

Recent newspaper coverage and television series have attempted to change the way we shop and eat, and the humble chicken has received its fair share of attention. As the living conditions of barn chickens, in particular, have been brought to our attention, people have begun to take more interest in how and where their chicken is reared and produced. It is no longer simply a case of picking up the first bird that comes to hand in the supermarket. We are now better informed and have more choice with regards to the meat we eat, as a result of which a greater number of people are choosing to buy free-range and organic chickens.

This is obviously good news for chickens, but the drawback is the price increase, which puts a dent in already-stretched grocery budgets. However, by using every last scrap of meat and then using the carcase to make stock, a medium chicken can provide more than one family meal, which makes economical sense as well as ensuring minimum food wastage.

Making savings

Instead of buying packaged chicken breasts, buy a whole bird and ask your butcher to joint it, or do it yourself. It won't cost much more and you will have all that extra meat.

•

When making a curry or stew, use thighs instead of breasts. They are a lot cheaper, and the denser, darker meat works well in slow-cooked recipes.

•

Even if roast chicken isn't on the dinner menu, this is a good cooking method to make the most of your bird. Once roasted, it is easy to separate the chicken pieces and remove the meat, dividing it up for meals.

•

If you have a lot of meat left over, cut it into smaller pieces and freeze it in individual portions. That way you can just take out what you need.

•

Make your chicken go further by using it for dishes such as curry or pasta, rather than simply serving whole chicken breasts.

stretching the budget

In the past, chicken was a luxury food that might have been eaten just once a week, or twice at most. Recently, however, we have grown accustomed to eating it almost on a daily basis, as the intensively reared modern bird has become an inexpensive, everyday item that we no longer hold in high regard. Quality rather than quantity should still matter, however, and while free-range chickens might cost a few pounds more, you should hopefully find it worth the investment in terms of flavour. There are a number of easy ways to make your chicken go further and ensure you get the most out of everything you buy.

don't waste a thing!

Roast chicken or turkey is one of our favourite meals, and probably the most popular festive dish, but it is also among the worst culprits when it comes to needless food waste. After a large meal and a glass or two of wine, wrapping up and saving any leftover meat might not be top of your priority list. However, it takes only a few minutes to trim away the remaining chicken or turkey meat and pop the carcase in a pan to boil. You then instantly have enough meat for another meal or two at your fingertips and a supply of delicious homemade stock. Cooked chicken can be kept for a couple of days in the refrigerator in an airtight container and used to make any number of dishes.

baby food

Even if you don't think there is sufficient meat left to make another meal, chicken is a great ingredient to add to baby and toddler meals. It will blend well with virtually any vegetables or other ingredients and you need only a few small pieces to make up a number of baby food portions. In fact, Sunday lunch is a great source of hassle-free baby food. Simply place any leftover (unseasoned) vegetables and meat in a food processor or liquidizer and blend until smooth. Add a little water, or vegetable cooking liquid, if the mixture is too dry.

Use it tonight

Risotto

Club sandwich

Chicken pasta

Coronation chicken

Curry

Soup

Enchiladas

Stir-fry

Chicken-fried rice

chicken noodle soup

serves 4

about 300 g (10 oz) leftover roast chicken, plus roast chicken bones

1 teaspoon concentrated chicken stock or 1 chicken stock cube

1 onion, cut in half

2 carrots, roughly chopped

750 ml (1¼ pints) water

2 tablespoons sweet chilli sauce

2 tablespoons Thai fish sauce (nam pla)

150 g (5 oz) dried egg noodles

300 g (10 oz) canned sweetcorn

2 tablespoons chopped parsley

salt and pepper

1 Place the chicken bones in a large saucepan with the concentrated chicken stock or stock cube, onion, carrots and water. Bring to the boil, then simmer for 1 hour. Strain the stock through a sieve and return it to the pan, then bring it back to the boil.

2 Add the sweet chilli sauce and fish sauce and season with salt and pepper, then add the noodles and cook until tender.

3 Place half the sweetcorn in a small food processor or liquidizer and blend with a little water until smooth. Stir the paste into the stock along with the rest of the sweetcorn and the roast chicken. Bring to the boil, then simmer for 1 minute before stirring in the parsley and serving.

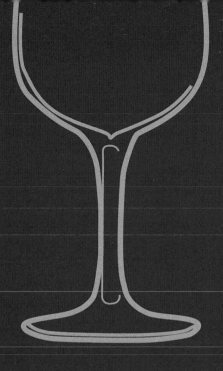

1 Heat the oil in a frying pan and gently fry the onion until translucent. Add the garlic and rice and fry for 2 minutes, coating the rice in the oil. Pour in the white wine and reduce down to just 1 tablespoon.

2 Add the hot stock, a large ladleful at a time, stirring until each addition has been absorbed into the rice. Continue adding stock in this way over a low heat for about 20 minutes until all the stock has been used up and the rice is creamy but still has some bite.

3 Add the chicken, vegetables, crème fraîche and Parmesan and stir well. Heat through thoroughly, so that the chicken is piping hot, then season with salt and pepper.

serves 4

2 tablespoons olive oil

1 small onion, finely chopped

1 garlic clove, crushed

375 g (12 oz) risotto rice

250 ml (8 fl oz) white wine

about 1.5 litres (2½ pints) hot chicken or vegetable stock

about 300 g (10 oz) leftover roast chicken

300 g (10 oz) cooked vegetables, such as butternut squash, peas, broccoli florets, sugar snap peas, broad beans, and so on

2 tablespoons crème fraîche

50 g (2 oz) Parmesan cheese, grated

salt and pepper

leftover chicken risotto

meat

Whether it's a delicious roast leg of lamb or a nice juicy steak, some of it always seems to find its way to the bin. Meat is by no means a money-saver when it comes to grocery shopping, so you really do need to use every last scrap to make it worth the investment.

cheaper cuts

One easy way to save some pennies is to buy less-popular cuts of meat. This doesn't mean scrimping on flavour or quality – it just means taking advantage of the lesser-known pieces of meat that are often overlooked by other people. These aren't always on display or available in supermarkets, so try using your local butcher and making the most of their specialized knowledge. Different cuts often require very different cooking times and techniques, so make sure you are aware of what works best before you start preparing the meal.

lamb

Scrag end This cut doesn't have the most appetizing name, but it tastes delicious in slow-cooked recipes such as stews. It is from the neck of the lamb so is not as tender as other cuts.

Shoulder Try pot-roasting a whole shoulder of lamb instead of the usual leg for Sunday lunch. You can also buy shoulder blade cuts, which can be cooked like any lamb chop.

beef

Brisket This is cut from beneath the ribs and is a tougher cut that requires a long cooking time. If cooked correctly, the meat will tenderize and the wonderful flavour will be imparted to the rest of the dish.

Skirt This is a cut from the diaphragm area and is ideal for braising. If you have a slow cooker, then this is a good cut to choose.

pork

Belly Pork belly can be made into streaky bacon or cooked as a whole cut of meat. It has wonderfully rich flavours when slowly roasted and basted.

Shoulder The hock is quite a fatty piece of meat so it is not usually served as a roast cut. However, the meat is tender and delicious and can be flaked away from the fat. It works really well in soups or combined with beans or vegetables to make a winter salad.

befriend your freezer

Another good way for the savvy shopper to make the most of meat is to look out for items that are reduced towards the end of the day in the supermarket. Make sure it is a cut and type of meat that you actually like and will use, then stock up for future use. Get it home quickly and put it in the freezer immediately. Alternatively, if you have bagged a bargain on lamb or beef mince, you could rustle up a couple of shepherd's pies or lasagnes and then freeze them. Freeze some as they are in large serving dishes, but make a few individual portions as well for those times when someone is at home alone and needs a quick, easy meal.

kids in the kitchen

Children love helping in the kitchen, and the messier they get the better, as far as they are concerned. Not only is cooking a great activity to while away a rainy afternoon, but it also helps to familiarize them with different ingredients and to gain a basic understanding of cooking techniques. While cakes and biscuits are always going to be top of the list, it's a good idea to introduce them to a broad range of recipes. Homemade burgers and meatballs are ideal, as they are easy to make, quick to cook and about as messy as you can get. Kids are also more likely to be interested in eating food that they have been involved in preparing, so make the whole experience as fun as possible and hopefully there'll be empty plates all round at dinnertime.

Top tips for cooking with kids

Get children into the habit of washing their hands before they start cooking. Always wash their hands again after handling meat.

•

Small burgers or patties are easier for little hands to make and also easier to eat.

•

Try to find a surface of the right height for them to work on — a children's table and chair set or toy box is ideal.

•

Place sheets of newspaper under the work area to catch the inevitable spills. You can just wrap them up and throw them straight in the bin once you've finished.

•

Let them 'accessorize' their own burgers — sauces, relishes and chopped salad will all add to the experience.

•

Mini pitta breads or rolls are perfect for kids as they are easy to hold.

slow cooking

If you are serious about making savings on your meat shopping, then the chances are you will be trying out some of the lesser-known cuts listed on pages 42–3. Many of these need a lengthy cooking time in order to break down the more fibrous meat and maximize the flavour. This in no way detracts from the quality of the meat: it simply means that certain cuts are denser than others. The more slowly they are cooked, the better the flavour, and in some cases the extra fat on the meat will add greatly to the final texture and taste of the dish. This will break down and melt during cooking and will combine with the other flavourings to produce a richer finish.

A slow cooker could be a great investment if you intend to cook these cuts on a regular basis. As well as being ideal for lengthy cooking times, it also means that you can set the dinner to cook before you leave home in the morning and it will be hot and ready to eat on your return. A slow cooker will also come in handy for making stews, soups and casseroles with any leftover meat. The other bonus is that you will be using less electricity than if you cooked in the oven, so you are being economical in two ways at once.

Tips for using a slow cooker

Keep the cooker out on the work surface: if it's packed away in the back of a cupboard, you won't use it.

•

Choose the right size for your needs: a small cooker won't be sufficient for family meals.

•

Make sure the cooker is preheated to the correct setting before you begin cooking.

•

Never fill the cooker right to the top, as there needs to be a little expansion space.

•

A slow cooker operates at a lower temperature than a regular oven, and if you remove the lid it will take a long time for the temperature to rise again.

•

Don't be tempted to add too much water or other liquid to the food. The cooker works by heating the food and retaining all the steam, so liquid will build up during the cooking time.

barbecue leftovers

The sun comes out, the barbecue is dusted off and you dash to the shops to stock up on burgers and sausages. This traditional British ritual is often so rare in the summer months, due to the highly unpredictable weather, that we tend to get a bit over-excited and buy far more food than we actually need. Once the barbecue is fired up, all this food inevitably gets cooked as barbecue frenzy takes over and we lose all concept of how much people are really going to eat. This means that much of it ends up in the refrigerator uneaten afterwards.

Using up barbecue leftovers tends to be more difficult than other types of food. It takes a little more imagination to think up ways to incorporate barbecued food into new dishes and it's unlikely that everyone will fancy cold sausages or burgers for the next two days. However, there are a number of delicious ways to ensure those bangers aren't binned. If you really don't think you will use up any leftovers the next day, then wrap the meat up well in separate portions and pop it in the freezer. Do this as soon as possible and try not to leave food hanging around in the heat.

Use it tonight: leftover roast meat

Spring rolls

Hot or cold sandwiches

Shepherd's pie

Stir-fry

Tacos or tortilla wraps

Chilli con carne

Curry

Meat and potato pie

Risotto

Use it tonight: leftover barbecue food

Sausage sandwiches

Spanish omelette with sausage

Sausage hotpot

Toad in the hole

Pizza topping (chopped sausage or burger)

Burgers in pittas with hummus

Chunky pasta sauce (chopped burgers)

Lamb curry (using kebabs)

Lamb stew

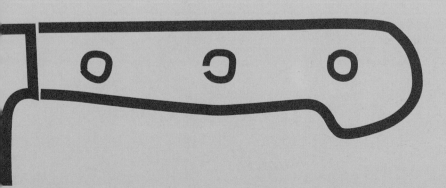

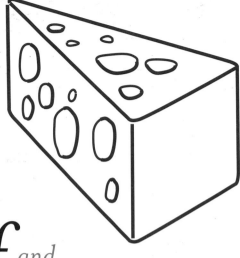

roast *beef* and *stilton* salad

serves 4

1 onion, cut into 12 wedges

3 tablespoons olive oil

2 tablespoons good-quality balsamic vinegar

4 slices of ciabatta bread, torn into pieces

about 500 g (1 lb) rare roast beef

150 g (5 oz) watercress

150 g (5 oz) Stilton cheese, crumbled

salt and pepper

1 Heat a griddle pan on a high heat. Toss the onion wedges in 1 tablespoon of the olive oil and season with salt and pepper, then griddle until softened and caramelized. Place in a large shallow bowl and pour the balsamic vinegar over, then toss together and leave to cool.

2 Heat another tablespoon of the oil in a frying pan and fry the ciabatta pieces until golden brown, then remove the croutons from the pan and set aside.

3 To prepare the salad, add the remaining oil, the beef and watercress to the onions and toss all the ingredients together, coating them in the oil and vinegar. Season with salt and pepper.

4 Divide the salad between 4 plates and scatter the Stilton and ciabatta croutons over the top.

1 Heat the oil in a saucepan and fry the onion and chillies until the onion is soft and translucent. Add the garlic and paprika and fry for a further minute. Add the wine and bring to the boil, then leave to bubble until the mixture is reduced by half. Add the tomatoes and return to the boil, then simmer for 10–15 minutes until the sauce is thick.

2 Stir in the beans, beef and mango chutney and warm through gently (overcooking the beef at this stage would make it tough).

3 Use a fork to mash up the avocado and mix in the crème fraîche. Season with salt and pepper and add enough lime juice to taste.

4 Place a couple of spoonfuls of the chilli on each tortilla and spoon some of the avocado mixture over the top. Roll the tortillas up, enclosing the filling.

serves 4

2 tablespoons olive oil or chilli oil

1 onion, finely chopped

2 large red chillies, deseeded and finely chopped

1 garlic clove, crushed

1 tablespoon smoked paprika

75 ml (3 fl oz) red wine

400 g (13 oz) can tomatoes

2 x 400 g (13 oz) cans kidney, butter or borlotti beans

about 400 g (13 oz) raw or cooked steak or roast beef, cut into 1 cm (½ inch) dice

1 tablespoon mango chutney

1 ripe avocado, stoned and peeled

4 tablespoons crème fraîche

juice of 1 lime

8 flour tortillas

salt and pepper

chunky beef and bean chilli fajitas

vegetables

Poor old leftover vegetables often have a bit of a rough deal when it comes to being used up. A couple of carrots or potatoes left over from dinner hardly seem worth saving, and so unless you have something specific in mind, they just get tossed in the bin. However, when you're watching your budget there is always a way to use up food.

the mighty vegetable

Vegetables are (or should be) an important part of our daily diet. They provide us with essential minerals and vitamins, as well as fibre and carbohydrates. The range of flavours, textures and colours means that, whether you are a committed meat eater or vegetarian, you can create wholesome, substantial and economical meals with any selection of fresh vegetables.

penny pinching

As the prices of everyday groceries continue to rise, many people have had to make cutbacks to their weekly food shop. Luxuries are limited and shoppers have become more aware of special offers and bulk buys. When once you might have popped packs of meat into the trolley without a second thought, now you may be thinking twice and saving those prime cuts for special occasions. This is where vegetables come in because they provide excellent value for money in terms of quantity and nutritional value. By combining them with a slow-release carbohydrate source, such as wholegrain rice or pasta, you can create an endless array of filling meals without spending too much.

Tips for buying and storing vegetables

Instead of buying all your vegetables at your weekly shop, try to buy them every day or two. Your vegetables will be really fresh and you should cut down on wastage, as you will be buying exactly what you need.

•

Most vegetables will keep fresher for longer if they are stored in the refrigerator. Remove any plastic packaging and keep them in the salad drawer, if possible, except for potatoes and onions, which like a cool, dark place.

•

Vegetables begin to lose their crispness and vitamin content as soon as they are harvested, so try to use them as soon as possible.

•

Stock up on a selection of frozen vegetables. Some produce, such as frozen peas, actually retain more goodness than the fresh version as they are frozen so quickly after harvest when the vitamin content is at its highest. Frozen vegetables make a good stand-by and can be added to stews, curries and soups.

•

Take your time when choosing vegetables and avoid anything with bruising. If you choose from a loose selection, you can look at them individually, whereas it can sometimes be difficult to spot damaged vegetables through packaging.

liven up your leftovers

If you do end up with a refrigerator full of cold vegetables, there are plenty of delicious meals that can be prepared with them.

vegetable pilaff Fry an onion in some olive oil, then add rice and stock to cover. Bring to the boil, then simmer until the rice is cooked through. Stir in any chopped vegetables.

curry Potatoes, sweet potatoes, beans and broccoli would all work well in a Thai or Indian curry. Use a bought sauce or make your own and simply heat the vegetables through before stirring in the sauce and serving with rice.

vegetable soup This is great for using up any leftover veg. Add seasoning to flavour the soup and either homemade stock or stock made from a cube. Tip the mixture into a food processor or liquidizer and blend to your preferred consistency.

ratatouille This is a delicious way to use up any leftover courgettes and peppers. Fry a chopped onion, add the vegetables to the pan and then stir in a can of chopped tomatoes. Leave to bubble and thicken, then serve with baked potatoes or as a side dish.

stir-fry A stir-fry is a quick and easy way to use up leftovers. Bulk it out with cashew nuts, prawns or diced chicken and serve with some rice or noodles.

vegetable omelette Peppers, mushrooms and potatoes are all good for making a quick omelette or Spanish omelette. Cook as you would normally, adding the chopped vegetables after the eggs.

pasta sauce Roughly chop leftover vegetables and add to some chopped tomatoes for a chunky sauce that will go well with penne or farfalle pasta.

Five ideas for leftover mash

Topping for shepherd's pie

Fish cakes

Croquettes

Potato patties

Potato soup

serves 4

2 tablespoons olive oil

1 small onion, finely chopped

1 red chilli, deseeded and finely chopped, or 1 teaspoon dried chilli flakes

1 garlic clove, crushed

1 teaspoon ground cumin

1 teaspoon ground coriander

1 tablespoon tomato purée

2 tomatoes, roughly chopped

300 g (10 oz) leftover cooked vegetables, such as peas, carrots, sweet potatoes, pumpkin, butternut squash, cauliflower, etc., cut into small pieces.

1 tablespoon mango chutney, plus extra to serve

8 sheets of filo pastry

50 g (2 oz) butter, melted

salt and pepper

natural yogurt, to serve

1 Heat the olive oil in a frying pan over a medium heat. Add the onion and chilli and fry until the onion is soft and translucent, then add the garlic, cumin and coriander. Fry for a further minute until the spices become fragrant.

2 Stir in the tomato purée and tomatoes and keep cooking until the tomatoes break down, adding a little water if necessary. Once the tomatoes have softened, cook the mixture for a few minutes to evaporate the water. Finally, add the vegetables, mango chutney and a little salt and pepper. Place this mixture in a bowl and set aside to cool.

3 Brush a sheet of filo pastry with a little melted butter and fold in half widthways, then brush again and fold in half lengthways to give you a long strip of pastry. Place a large spoonful of the vegetable mixture at the end of the pastry strip in the corner. Fold the other corner over, covering the filling with a triangle of pastry. Keep folding the pastry, moving up the strip, to give you a triangular parcel. Brush the end with a little butter to seal the edge, then brush the outside of the samosa and place on a baking tray. Repeat with the rest of the ingredients.

4 Bake in a preheated oven, 180°C (350°F) Gas Mark 4, for 15–20 minutes until golden brown. Serve with yogurt and mango chutney.

spicy *vegetable* samosas

tempura
vegetables

serves 4

500 g (1 lb) cooked vegetables in large pieces, such as broccoli or cauliflower florets, courgettes, carrots, aubergines, onion rings, etc.

50 g (2 oz) flour, for dusting

vegetable oil, for deep-frying

1 lime, cut into wedges, to garnish

sweet chilli sauce, to serve

for the batter

150 g (5 oz) self-raising flour

1 tablespoon cornflour

125 ml (4 fl oz) sparkling water

salt and pepper

1 Make the batter by placing the flour, cornflour and a good pinch of salt and pepper in a large bowl. Using a fork, stir in enough sparkling water to make a batter. It should be the thickness of double cream. Do not over-stir the batter – there should still be small lumps of flour in it.

2 In a large, heavy-based saucepan or wok, heat sufficient oil for deep-frying to 180°C (350°F), or until a cube of bread browns in 30 seconds.

3 Toss the vegetables in the flour and then dip in the batter. Fry the vegetables in batches until golden brown, then remove from the oil and drain on kitchen paper. Sprinkle the tempura with a little salt, garnish with lime wedges and serve with sweet chilli sauce.

fruit

Despite filling up our fruit bowls and trying to stick to those good intentions of eating the government-recommended five portions of fruit and veg every day, it seems we just can't stop throwing out perfectly good pieces of fruit. It sits there looking at us day after day and we still don't get around to eating it.

health boost

Fresh fruit is one of the best ways to get an instant vitamin hit, and with so many varieties of fruit available in supermarkets and greengrocers, there's no excuse for not having enough choice. Fruit is quick and easy to eat and is far healthier (and usually cheaper) than a packet of crisps or a chocolate bar.

storing fruit

Fruit is so versatile that it can be eaten at any meal of the day. It can be used in sweet and savoury dishes and every type of recipe from starters to desserts. It can be eaten raw or cooked in a variety of different ways.

Different types of fruit are better suited to different storage methods in order to get the most out of them. Some varieties are best eaten within a few days of purchase whilst others will keep for much longer, under the correct conditions. Raspberries, blackcurrants and other small berries won't stay fresh for very long but they freeze really well. Spread them in a single layer on a baking tray and freeze until firm. Transfer them to a freezer bag or container and they won't stick together. You can then use as few or as many as you need, straight from the freezer, for dishes such as crumbles and smoothies.

Other fruit, such as rhubarb and apples, freezes better if it has been cooked first. Simply chop into small pieces, sweeten with a little sugar and add a dash of orange juice, then simmer gently until the fruit is softened. Alternatively, freeze raw but dipped in a sugar syrup first (see page 158).

Getting five a day

A glass of juice counts as one serving, so if you have a bowl of oranges that you can't seem to get through, turn them into some freshly squeezed juice for breakfast.

•

Take fruit into work and keep it out on your desk. When boredom strikes you can tuck in.

•

Pack fruit in kids' lunch boxes or carry some to give as a snack when you are out. You can vary it by putting a handful of grapes in a little container or a kiwi cut in half with a spoon to scoop out the flesh.

•

Swap your usual mid-morning biscuit or mid-afternoon cake for a handful of raisins or some chopped fresh fruit.

You often find that you are waiting for fruit to reach its optimum ripeness and then it is a race against time to eat it before it begins deteriorating. To speed up the ripening process, put a banana in the same bowl; likewise ensure the bowl is banana free if you want the fruit to last longer. Keep an eye on the fruit bowl and quickly remove any fruit with bruises, as these will spread fast and impact on the other fruit. This doesn't mean the fruit should be discarded, of course: just cut away the bruised area and the rest will be fine to eat.

Getting fruity

You can make a fruit salad out of virtually any variety of fruit, and this is great for using up odds and ends. Keep it covered in a bowl in the refrigerator for a day or so and use on breakfast cereal, as a quick snack or for dessert, served with yogurt.

•

Ripe bananas are just begging to be turned into a delicious smoothie, and natural yogurt and a dash of honey are the only other ingredients you need.

•

Make a fruit compote from apples or pears: simply simmer in a little orange juice for a couple of minutes. This can then be used in crumbles or served with other desserts. Other compotes can be made from combinations of fruit, such as autumn fruits or summer berries, which can then be served with cream or ice cream. If the juice of a lemon is added, plus a little more sugar to balance the sharpness, the compote can be kept in sterilized jars for 3-6 months.

•

Turn a glut of summer berries, plums or apples into homemade jam and chutney.

•

Become a forager and collect blackberries while out on a country walk. Blackberry and apple crumble tastes so much sweeter when you've picked the ingredients yourself.

Make it tonight happy ever afters

Banana split
Poached pears
Eton mess
Raspberry coulis
Pineapple upside-down cake
Fruit trifle
Summer pudding

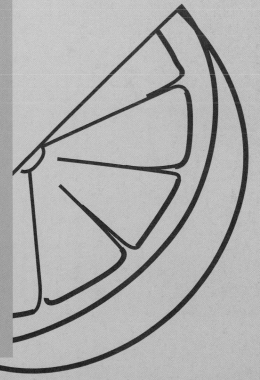

serves 6

125 g (4 oz) caster sugar

50 g (2 oz) butter

4–5 apples or pears, peeled, halved and cored, or 4–5 peaches or 8–10 plums, halved and stoned

1 sheet ready-rolled puff pastry

ice cream, custard or thick double cream, to serve

tarte *tatin*

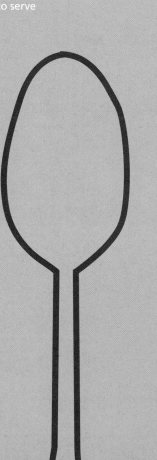

1 Heat a nonstick frying pan with heatproof handle over a medium heat. Sprinkle the sugar over the base of the pan in an even layer and leave to melt and become golden brown, swirling the pan to melt any islands of sugar rather than stirring. Remove the pan from the heat and stir in the butter. If the sugar starts to become solid, do not worry as it will melt again in the oven.

2 Place the prepared fruit cut side up in the pan. Cover the fruit with the pastry (this may need rolling out a little more), tucking it down at the sides of the pan.

3 Bake in a preheated oven, 180°C (350°F), Gas Mark 4, for 15–20 minutes until golden brown.

4 Leave to cool for a few minutes before carefully inverting the tart on to a large plate. Serve with ice cream, custard or thick double cream.

1 Place the fruit in a saucepan with the lemon rind. Cover and bring to the boil, then simmer for 4–5 minutes, or until the fruit has softened but is still whole. Add sugar to taste. Remove from the heat and leave to cool slightly.

2 Mix together the eggs, cream and sugar in a shallow bowl. Heat a frying pan over a high heat, add half the butter and oil to the pan and heat until bubbling. Dip the bread in the cream and egg mixture, coating it well, and allow a little to soak into the bread.

3 Fry in batches for 2 minutes on each side, or until golden brown, keeping the first batch warm while you cook the second. Serve with the warm compote and cream.

french toast with poached fruit compote

serves 4

for the fruit compote

500 g (1 lb) fruit such as apples or pears, peeled, cored and sliced, plums, peaches or nectarines, stoned and sliced, or fresh/frozen berries, hulled if necessary

finely grated rind of 1 lemon

about 50 g (2 oz) caster sugar

for the french toast

2 eggs, beaten

150 ml (¼ pint) double cream

2 tablespoons caster sugar

50 g (2 oz) unsalted butter

1 tablespoon vegetable oil

4 thick slices of bread

budget
basics

family meals with flair

It's the easiest thing in the world to do, and we probably all do it to a greater or lesser degree: cook the same meals, week in, week out, using the same ingredients and not even wondering if they're good value or even good for us. So now's the time to stand back and take a fresh look at how you feed your family; just a glance at the fantastic recipes here will reawaken your old enthusiasm for cooking. Flavoursome and hearty soups, great meat and poultry ideas, fantastic fish dishes, imaginative vegetable creations and tempting desserts, all made with economical ingredients and cooked from scratch, will make sure you save money and calories, and give your family's tastebuds a treat.

light
meals

minestrone
soup

serves 6

2 tablespoons olive oil, plus extra
for drizzling

1 onion, chopped

3 carrots, chopped

3 celery sticks, chopped

2 garlic cloves, thinly sliced

410 g (13½ oz) can cannellini beans,
drained and rinsed

400 g (13 oz) can plum tomatoes or
6 fresh tomatoes, skinned and chopped

150 g (5 oz) peas or broad beans

1 large potato, peeled and diced

2 courgettes, diced

1.5 litres (2½ pints) chicken or
vegetable stock

150 g (5 oz) spinach, thick stalks
removed, shredded, or cabbage,
cored and shredded

75 g (3 oz) small dried pasta shapes

salt and pepper

to serve

freshly grated Parmesan or
pecorino cheese

ready-made pesto

1. Heat the oil in a large saucepan and gently fry the onion, carrots and celery for 5 minutes. Add the garlic and fry for a further 2 minutes.

2. Add the beans, tomatoes, peas or broad beans, potato, courgettes and stock to the pan. Bring slowly to the boil, then cover and simmer gently for about 1 hour, or until all the vegetables are tender.

3. Add the spinach or cabbage and the pasta and stir gently. Return to the boil, then cover and simmer for 10 minutes, or until the pasta is cooked. Season to taste.

4. Ladle into warm soup bowls, drizzle with extra olive oil and serve with the Parmesan or pecorino and some pesto.

1 Heat the oil in a large saucepan, add the onions and fry gently for 5 minutes, or until softened and golden brown. Add the garlic, if using, and cook gently for 1 minute.

2 Add the red peppers and 1 of the courgettes and fry for 5–8 minutes, or until softened and brown, then add the stock or water. Bring to the boil, then cover and simmer gently for 20 minutes.

3 When the vegetables are tender, tip the mixture into a food processor or liquidizer and blend until smooth, in batches if necessary. Alternatively, rub through a sieve. Return to the pan and season to taste with salt and pepper, then reheat the soup.

4 Ladle into warm soup bowls and top with the remaining chopped courgette, a swirl of yogurt or cream and some chives.

bright red
pepper soup

serves 4

2 tablespoons groundnut or olive oil

2 onions, finely chopped

1 garlic clove, crushed (optional)

3 red peppers, cored, deseeded and roughly chopped

2 courgettes, roughly chopped

900 ml (1½ pints) vegetable stock or water

salt and pepper

to garnish

natural yogurt or double cream

snipped chives

carrot and *lentil* soup

serves 4

250 g (8 oz) split red lentils

1 leek, trimmed, cleaned and sliced

2 large carrots, sliced

1 celery stick, sliced

1 garlic clove, crushed (optional)

1 bay leaf

1.2 litres (2 pints) vegetable stock

½ teaspoon cayenne pepper

pepper

to garnish

natural yogurt

snipped chives or
    finely chopped parsley

1 Place all the ingredients except the pepper in a large saucepan. Bring to the boil, then cover and simmer for 20–25 minutes, or until the lentils and vegetables are all tender.

2 Allow the soup to cool slightly and remove the bay leaf. Tip the mixture into a food processor or liquidizer and blend until smooth, in batches if necessary. Alternatively, rub through a sieve. Pour the soup into a clean saucepan, season with pepper and heat through.

3 Ladle into warm soup bowls and garnish with a spoonful of yogurt and a sprinkling of chives or parsley.

courgette, *sun–dried* tomato and *ricotta* *flan*

serves 4

for the pastry

250 g (8 oz) plain flour, plus extra
for dusting

pinch of salt

125 g (4 oz) chilled butter, diced

2–3 tablespoons iced water

for the filling

2 tablespoons olive oil

1 small onion, thinly sliced

2 courgettes, thinly sliced

50 g (2 oz) drained sun-dried
tomatoes in oil, sliced

250 g (8 oz) ricotta or curd cheese

2 tablespoons milk

2 eggs, beaten

4 tablespoons chopped fresh herbs
(basil, rosemary, sage, thyme)

12 black olives, pitted and halved
(optional)

salt and pepper

1 To make the pastry, sift the flour and salt into a large mixing bowl, add the butter and rub in with the fingertips until the mixture resembles fine breadcrumbs. Gradually add enough cold water to bind the ingredients. On a lightly floured surface, knead the dough briefly until smooth, then wrap in clingfilm and chill for 30 minutes.

2 Roll out the pastry on a lightly floured surface and use to line a 23 cm (9 inch) flan tin. Prick the base with a fork and chill for 20 minutes. Line the pastry case with foil and baking beans and cook in a preheated oven, 200°C (400°F), Gas Mark 6, for 10 minutes. Remove the foil and beans and bake for a further 10–12 minutes until the pastry is crisp and golden.

3 Heat the oil in a frying pan, add the onion and courgettes and fry gently for 5–6 minutes until lightly golden. Scatter over the base of the pastry case and top with the sun-dried tomatoes.

4 Put the ricotta or curd cheese, milk, eggs, herbs and salt and pepper into a bowl and beat together. Spread this topping over the courgette mixture and scatter the olives on top, if using. Bake for 30–35 minutes until firm and golden.

serves 6

for the pastry

250 g (8 oz) plain flour, plus extra for dusting

pinch of salt

125 g (4 oz) chilled butter, diced

1 egg yolk

2–3 tablespoons iced water

for the filling

50 g (2 oz) butter

150 g (5 oz) smoked bacon, cut into small pieces

350 ml (12 fl oz) double cream

3 eggs

¼ teaspoon freshly grated nutmeg

salt and pepper

1 To make the pastry, sift the flour and salt into a large mixing bowl, add the butter and rub in with the fingertips until the mixture resembles fine breadcrumbs. Gradually add the egg yolk and enough cold water to bind the ingredients. On a lightly floured surface, knead the dough briefly until smooth, then wrap in clingfilm and chill for 30 minutes.

2 On a lightly floured surface, roll out the pastry and use to line a 23 cm (9 inch) flan tin.

3 Melt one-half of the butter in a frying pan and cook the bacon gently until lightly coloured. Sprinkle the cooked bacon over the base of the pastry case and dot with the remaining butter.

4 Put the cream and eggs in a bowl and whisk together, then add the grated nutmeg and seasoning. Pour this mixture over the bacon. Bake in a preheated oven, 200°C (400°F) Gas Mark 6, for 30 minutes, or until set and golden brown. Serve warm.

quiche
lorraine

spanish omelette

1 Heat the oil in a 20–23 cm (8–9 inch) heavy nonstick frying pan and add the potatoes and onion. Cover the pan and cook over a low heat for about 30 minutes until the potatoes are tender, but not browned, lifting and turning them occasionally.

2 Beat the eggs in a large shallow bowl until they are slightly foamy and season with salt and pepper. Once the vegetables are soft and well cooked, lift them out of the pan with a slotted spoon and drain in a colander, reserving the oil. Add the potatoes and onion to the beaten eggs, pressing them down well so that they are completely covered. If possible, leave to stand for about 15 minutes.

3 Wipe the pan clean, then heat about 2–3 tablespoons of the reserved oil over a medium heat. Add the egg and vegetable mixture and quickly spread it out with a palette knife. Reduce the heat and cook very gently, shaking the pan occasionally to prevent the tortilla from sticking. After about 15 minutes, when the mixture begins to brown underneath and shrink slightly from the edge of the pan, remove the pan from the heat.

4 Invert the tortilla on to a flat plate, slightly larger than the pan, then heat another tablespoon of oil in the pan and slide the tortilla back for about 3–4 minutes to brown the other side. (Alternatively, simply place the pan under a preheated medium grill, wrapping the handle in kitchen foil first if it is not heatproof, and cook until the surface is golden brown.) The tortilla should be golden brown on the outside but still moist and juicy inside. Transfer to a plate and serve hot or cold.

serves 4

150 ml (¼ pint) olive oil

4 large potatoes, peeled and cut into 3 mm (⅛ inch) slices

1 large onion, thinly sliced

4–5 large eggs

salt and pepper

lunchbox *basics*

When you're watching your budget, the easiest way to eat well without breaking the bank is to eat at home. But what about when it comes to meals outside the home? If you're out and about all day, you can find you've spent an awful lot of money just buying a basic lunch or a few snacks. The easiest and cheapest solution is to take your lunch with you. Whether you take the makings of a picnic lunch, such as rolls, sandwich fillings and fruit, to work to keep you going through the week, or make a more exotic and varied selection of picnics to enjoy fresh each day, is up to you.

Sensational sandwiches and wraps

A tasty filling slapped between two slices of bread is the easiest lunch to throw in a box, but you don't need to stop with the basics. Try getting creative with some of these fun and funky ideas for fillings and breads.

Chicken salad pitta Split a pitta bread down the side to create a pocket, then fill it with a mixture of leftover roast chicken chopped into bite-sized pieces, diced green pepper and celery, a few sultanas and a good dollop of mayonnaise.

Spicy hummus wrap Spread a flour tortilla with hummus, top with grated carrot and a good drizzle of sweet chilli sauce, then roll up.

Chunky sausage sandwich Lightly butter two thick slices of wholemeal bread, and spread a good layer of sweet and spicy chutney on one slice. Top with slices of cooked, leftover sausages and top with the second slice of bread.

Double-decker ploughman's For anyone who's extra hungry, lightly butter three slices of bread. Spread the first slice with pickle, top with slices of cheese, tomato and lettuce, then top with a second layer of bread and more pickle, cheese and salad before topping with the final slice of bread.

Brie and cranberry baguette Split open a medium baguette and lightly butter. Top with slices of Brie and lashings of cranberry jelly.

Mozzarella, tomato and pesto ciabatta Cut a good-sized chunk of ciabatta, split in half and lightly butter. Top with slices of mozzarella and tomato and drizzle over plenty of pesto.

Bacon, avocado and roast pepper bap Fill a lightly buttered bap with rashers of bacon, slices of avocado and leftover roast peppers. (If you don't have leftover roast peppers, tomato makes a good alternative.)

Fabulous lunchbox fillers

A packed lunch doesn't have to mean sandwiches and wraps. There are so many other great things to throw into a lunchbox instead, and many of them can be made using the leftovers from yesterday's supper – so they're economical as well as tasty. Try a wedge of Spanish tortilla or Italian frittata with cherry tomatoes and slices of cucumber; hot soup from a flask, with a crusty bread roll; pasta, rice, bean and couscous salads; and hummus or smoked mackerel pâté with wedges of pitta and vegetable sticks.

Save on snacks and drinks

Buying a bottle of smoothie or a carton of juice every day soon adds up, so why not just drink tap water instead? It's good for you and it's absolutely free.

•

Don't just take a packed lunch with you — be prepared with snacks as well. Fresh and dried fruit, nuts and seeds, and vegetable sticks all make great, healthy snacks to munch on during the day. However, don't be tempted by the expensive individual packs of dried fruit, nuts and seeds from the supermarket: instead, make up your own bag of goodies from larger, more economical packs.

•

Has that take-out coffee from the deli become a daily habit? Why not invest in a cafetière or coffee pot and some good-quality ground coffee so you can make your own instead? It might seem like an extravagance buying the coffee pot, but work out how much money you spend on your daily brew in a paper cup. If you make your own, you'll find you've saved the money back in only a couple of weeks. And what about that muffin or cookie you pick up to go with your cuppa? The same treat from a supermarket is a fraction of the cost, so why not buy enough in your weekly shop and take them into the office to enjoy with your home-brewed coffee?

serves 4

250 g (8 oz) floury potatoes, peeled and diced

2 x 200 g (7 oz) cans tuna in olive oil, drained and flaked

50 g (2 oz) Cheddar cheese, grated

4 spring onions, finely chopped

1 small garlic clove, crushed

2 teaspoons dried thyme

1 egg, beaten

½ teaspoon cayenne pepper

4 tablespoons seasoned flour

vegetable oil, for frying

salt and pepper

to serve

mixed green salad

mayonnaise

tuna fish cakes

1 Cook the potatoes in a saucepan of lightly salted boiling water for 10 minutes, or until tender. Drain well, mash and cool slightly.

2 Beat the tuna, Cheddar, spring onions, garlic, thyme and egg into the mashed potato and season to taste with cayenne, salt and pepper.

3 Divide the mixture into 4 and shape into thick patties. Dust with seasoned flour and fry in a shallow layer of vegetable oil for 5 minutes on each side, until crisp and golden. Serve the fish cakes hot with a mixed green salad and mayonnaise.

spicy fried sardines

serves 4

vegetable oil, for deep-frying

750 g (1½ lb) large, fresh sardines, cleaned

125 g (4 oz) seasoned flour

4 tablespoons olive oil

5 shallots, sliced

125 ml (4 fl oz) white wine vinegar

4 garlic cloves, crushed

large handful of mint leaves, finely chopped

rind and juice of 1 lemon

½ teaspoon crushed dried chillies

salt and pepper

1 In a large, heavy-based saucepan or wok, heat sufficient oil for deep-frying to 180–190°C (350–375°F), or until a cube of bread browns in 30 seconds.

2 Dip the sardines into the seasoned flour to coat evenly and fry in the hot oil for 2 minutes, or until golden. Remove and place on a tray lined with kitchen paper to absorb the excess oil. Keep warm.

3 Heat 1 tablespoon of the olive oil in a saucepan, add the shallots and sauté for 5 minutes, then add the vinegar and cook until nearly one-half of it has evaporated.

4 Transfer the sardines to a warmed serving dish. Add the remaining olive oil, the garlic, mint, lemon rind and juice and dried chillies to the onion mixture and cook for 1 minute. Spoon the sauce over the sardines and season with salt and pepper. Serve hot or at room temperature.

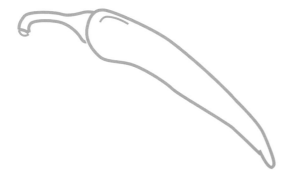

red pepper and bean cakes

serves 4

75 g (3 oz) French beans, trimmed and roughly chopped

4 tablespoons groundnut or vegetable oil

1 red pepper, cored, deseeded and diced

4 garlic cloves, crushed

2 teaspoons mild chilli powder

410 g (13½ oz) can red kidney beans, drained and rinsed

75 g (3 oz) fresh white breadcrumbs

1 egg yolk

flour, for dusting

salt and pepper

for the lemon mayonnaise

4 tablespoons mayonnaise

finely grated rind of 1 lemon

1 teaspoon lemon juice

salt and pepper

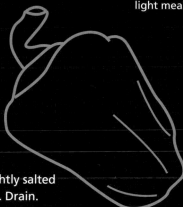

1 Blanch the French beans in a saucepan of lightly salted boiling water for 1–2 minutes until softened. Drain.

2 Meanwhile, heat one-half of the oil in a frying pan and gently fry the pepper, garlic and chilli powder for 2 minutes.

3 Transfer the mixture to a food processor or liquidizer and add the red kidney beans, breadcrumbs and egg yolk. Blend very briefly until the ingredients are coarsely chopped. Add the drained French beans, season to taste with salt and pepper and process until the ingredients are just combined. Turn the mixture into a bowl and divide into 8 portions. Using lightly floured hands, shape the portions into 8 patties.

4 To make the lemon mayonnaise, mix the mayonnaise with the lemon rind and juice and season to taste with salt and pepper.

5 Heat the remaining oil in a large frying pan and fry the cakes for about 3 minutes on each side until crisp and golden. Serve with the lemon mayonnaise.

boston *baked* *beans*

serves 2

1 tablespoon vegetable oil

1 small red onion, finely chopped

2 celery sticks, finely chopped

1 garlic clove, crushed

200 g (7 oz) can chopped tomatoes

150 ml (¼ pint) vegetable stock

1 tablespoon dark soy sauce

1 tablespoon soft dark brown sugar

2 teaspoons Dijon mustard

410 g (13½ oz) can mixed beans, drained and rinsed

2 tablespoons chopped parsley

1 Heat the oil in a heavy-based saucepan. Add the onion and cook over a low heat for 5 minutes, or until softened. Add the celery and garlic and cook for a further 1–2 minutes.

2 Add the tomatoes, stock and soy sauce. Bring to the boil, then simmer briskly for about 15 minutes, or until the sauce begins to thicken.

3 Add the sugar, mustard and beans. Continue to cook for a further 5 minutes, or until the beans are heated through. Stir in the chopped parsley and serve.

stuffed *vegetables*
with cheesy couscous

serves 4

1. Put the tomatoes and peppers, cut sides up, in a large, shallow, ovenproof dish, drizzle with the oil and season with a little salt and pepper. Bake in a preheated oven, 200°C (400 °F), Gas Mark 6, for 20 minutes until softened.

2. Meanwhile, put the couscous in a bowl, pour the boiling water over and leave to stand for 10 minutes until the water is absorbed. Fluff up the couscous with a fork and stir in the spring onions, basil, mozzarella, Parmesan and chickpeas. Season to taste.

3. Remove the vegetables from the oven and spoon the couscous mixture into the hollows. Return the dish to the oven for a further 8–10 minutes until the vegetables have heated through and the mozzarella has melted. Serve warm.

2 beefsteak tomatoes, halved horizontally and deseeded

2 red, orange or yellow peppers, halved, cored and deseeded

2 tablespoons olive oil

175 g (6 oz) couscous

300 ml (½ pint) boiling water

½ bunch of spring onions, chopped

small handful of basil leaves, torn into pieces

125 g (4 oz) mozzarella cheese, drained and chopped

25 g (1 oz) Parmesan cheese, freshly grated

410 g (13½ oz) can chickpeas, drained and rinsed

salt and pepper

serves 6

4 tablespoons olive oil

2 onions, finely chopped

2 garlic cloves, crushed (optional)

1 aubergine, diced

500 g (1 lb) courgettes, diced

3 red, 1 yellow and 2 green peppers, cored, deseeded and roughly chopped

2 x 400 g (13 oz) cans chopped tomatoes

2 teaspoons dried mixed herbs

50 g (2 oz) dried breadcrumbs

25 g (1 oz) Cheddar cheese, grated

1 tablespoon freshly grated Parmesan cheese

salt and pepper

1 Heat the oil in a large saucepan and gently fry the onions until soft and golden brown. Add the garlic, if using, and cook for a further 1 minute.

2 Add the aubergine and courgettes and fry until soft and beginning to brown, then add the peppers and stir to coat in the oil. Cook for 5 minutes until the peppers have softened. Add the tomatoes and bring to a fast boil, then add the herbs and season with salt and pepper. Half-cover the pan and simmer for 10 minutes.

3 Spoon the ratatouille mixture into a large ovenproof dish and level the top. Mix the breadcrumbs with the Cheddar and Parmesan and sprinkle on top. Bake in a preheated oven, 220°C (425°F), Gas Mark 7, for 20–25 minutes, or until the breadcrumb mixture is golden brown and bubbling.

ratatouille gratin

main
meals

chicken and spinach
potato pie

serves 4

2 tablespoons sunflower or
   vegetable oil

1 onion, chopped

3 garlic cloves, sliced

4 cm (1½ inch) piece of fresh root
   ginger, peeled and finely shredded

6 boneless, skinless chicken thighs,
   cut into chunks

300 ml (½ pint) chicken stock

75 g (3 oz) creamed coconut

875 g (1¾ lb) potatoes,
   peeled and cut into pieces

5 tablespoons semi-skimmed milk

150 g (5 oz) spinach,
   thick stalks removed

freshly grated nutmeg

salt and pepper

broccoli or peas, to serve

1. Heat the oil in a large frying pan. Add the onion, garlic, ginger and chicken and fry gently for about 5 minutes until the chicken just begins to colour.

2. Add the stock and creamed coconut and bring just to the boil, then simmer, stirring gently to blend the coconut into the liquid. Cover and simmer for a further 10 minutes.

3. Meanwhile, cook the potatoes in a saucepan of lightly salted boiling water for 10 minutes, or until tender. Drain, then return to the pan and mash with the milk.

4. Pile the spinach on top of the chicken mixture and cover with a lid. Leave to cook gently for 1–2 minutes until the spinach has wilted. Add plenty of nutmeg and a little salt and pepper, and stir the spinach in.

5. Turn the mixture into a 1.8 litre (3 pint) pie dish. Top with the mashed potato and rough up the surface with a fork. Bake the pie in a preheated oven, 180°C (350°F), Gas Mark 4, for about 30 minutes until the surface is pale golden. Serve with a green vegetable, such as broccoli or peas.

balancing your *budget*

For many people, particularly those of us who aren't too good with numbers, the idea of balancing a budget can seem a fearsome thing. However, it doesn't need to be scary – and listed below are some different approaches you can take along with some tips for making managing your budget easier.

How much did this meal cost?

An easy way to start off planning a budget is to work out how much you have to spend on each meal (or on each day's food). However, this can be a slightly tricky process because you'll need to do some careful calculation to turn the ingredients you buy into the ingredients you use to make a specific dish. For example: if you make a meal of pasta with tomato sauce for four, first, you'll need to work out how much all your basic ingredients cost:

- 325 g (11 oz) dried pasta (approximately ⅓ of a 1 kg/2 lb bag of pasta)
- 1 onion
- 2 garlic cloves (approximately ⅛ of a garlic bulb)
- 2 x 400 g (13 oz) cans of tomatoes
- 15 g (½ oz) bunch of fresh basil (or about ½ pot fresh basil or 2 handfuls of basil leaves from the garden)
- 2 tbsp olive oil (approximately 1/16 of a 500 ml/ 17 fl oz bottle of olive oil)
- 50 g (2 oz) Parmesan (⅕ of a 250 g/8 oz piece of Parmesan)

And if you're working out a budget per person, you'll then need to divide your total cost by four.

As you can see, working out the cost of a meal is a fiddly business, and this example doesn't even take into account whether there is any waste (for example, did you use up the rest of the piece of Parmesan in other dishes, or did you forget all about it and end up throwing some away?) or seasonings such as salt and pepper, the cost of which are minimal for one dish, but that you need to buy once in a while.

Looking at the bigger picture

A simpler way to look after your budget is to consider your food costs over a week, or, better still, a month. That way, you get a much more realistic idea of how much you're spending. For example, you won't be worrying about exactly how many pence-worth of olive oil or black pepper you spent in a single meal, or have to keep another list of ingredients that you ended up throwing away: 1 onion, 2 cloves of garlic, 25 g (1 oz) Parmesan cheese...

Approaching your budget this way also allows you more flexibility as to what you eat for every meal. It can be helpful to start off with an idea of how much you want to spend on each meal, but by looking at your budget as a whole rather than per meal, you'll find you have much more flexibility. For example, if you want to splash out on a special meal or dinner party, you can cut back on other meals, making cheaper choices using economical, everyday ingredients.

Splashing out and cutting back

For most people, their meals throughout the week are a mixture of more extravagant and then more frugal fare according to their schedule and lifestyle. Below are some ideas that most of us can follow to accommodate a few splurges during the week.

• For those who enjoy a really hearty family meal in the evening, make more economical choices during the rest of the day, such as cereal for breakfast, soup or leftovers for lunch, and healthy but economical snacks such as toast with peanut butter, a banana or a yogurt.
• If you like a blow-out breakfast at the weekends, don't feel you need to give up your fry-up or Continental pastries with freshly brewed coffee. Just save up during the week with more economical choices such as porridge.
• When you're entertaining, work it into your budget and plan economical meals for the rest of the week such as pasta- and rice-based dishes, and baked potatoes with tasty fillings.
• If you want to make a luxurious dessert or a birthday cake but your budget won't allow it, how about cutting out cheaper desserts during the rest of the week so you can afford a really special one? It'll help your waistline, too!
• Enjoy a Sunday roast? This is a great way to get the family together for a proper meal, so don't give up on the idea. Why not slip in some hearty vegetarian meals during the week to accommodate the cost of the roast?

chicken and lemon paella

serves 2

4 teaspoons olive oil

300 g (10 oz) boneless, skinless chicken thighs, diced

1 onion, sliced

2 garlic cloves, crushed

1 red pepper, cored, deseeded and roughly chopped

75 g (3 oz) easy-cook white long-grain rice

2 tablespoons dry sherry

250 ml (8 fl oz) chicken stock

200 g (7 oz) frozen peas

grated rind and juice of 1 lemon

salt and pepper

to garnish

thyme sprigs

lemon wedges

1 Heat one-half of the oil in a frying pan over a medium heat and cook the chicken for 4–6 minutes, or until golden, then remove from the pan.

2 Heat the remaining oil and cook the onion over a medium heat for 10 minutes until soft, then add the garlic and red pepper and cook for a further 3 minutes.

3 Stir in the rice and pour in the sherry and stock, then return the chicken to the pan. Turn the heat to low and simmer for 10–15 minutes.

4 Add the peas and cook for a further 2–3 minutes, or until the liquid has evaporated. Stir in the lemon rind and juice, then season to taste with salt and pepper. Garnish with thyme sprigs and lemon wedges.

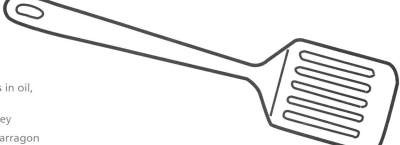

serves 4

sun-dried tomato halves in oil,
  drained and chopped

500 g (1 lb) minced turkey

1 tablespoon chopped tarragon

½ red onion, finely chopped

¼ teaspoon paprika

¼ teaspoon salt

4 slices of smoked pancetta or
  rindless streaky bacon, halved

to serve

4 ciabatta rolls

shredded radicchio

shredded Cos lettuce

1 Place the sun-dried tomatoes, turkey and tarragon in
a food processor or liquidizer and blend until smooth.
Spoon the mixture into a bowl and stir in the onion,
paprika and salt, mixing well.

2 Divide the mixture into 4 equal portions and shape into
patties. Stretch 2 strips of pancetta or bacon over each
burger and secure with cocktail sticks soaked in water
for 30 minutes.

3 Cook the burgers under a preheated medium-hot grill
for 20–25 minutes, turning frequently. Serve immediately
in the ciabatta rolls with shredded lettuce.

turkey burgers
with
sun–dried tomatoes

ham *and* egg linguini

serves 2

100 g (3½ oz) thinly sliced ham
2 spring onions
125 g (4 oz) dried linguine
2 eggs
salt and pepper

for the mustard dressing

3 tablespoons chopped flat leaf parsley
1 tablespoon coarse-grain mustard
2 teaspoons lemon juice
good pinch of caster sugar
3 tablespoons olive oil
salt and pepper

1 Mix together the ingredients for the mustard dressing. Roll up the ham and slice it as thinly as possible. Trim the spring onions and cut them lengthways into thin shreds, then cut into 5 cm (2 inch) lengths.

2 Cook the pasta in a saucepan of lightly salted water for 6–8 minutes, or until just tender. Add the spring onions and cook for a further 30 seconds. Meanwhile, put the eggs in a small saucepan and just cover with cold water. Bring to the boil and cook for 4 minutes.

3 Drain the pasta and spring onions and return to the pan. Stir in the ham and the mustard dressing and pile on to warm plates. Shell and halve the eggs and place on top.

1 Heat the oil in a large saucepan, add the onion, garlic and red pepper and fry for 2–3 minutes until they begin to soften. Add the sausages and continue to cook for 5 minutes until browned all over.

2 Lightly crush one-half of the beans with the back of a fork and add to the pan with the remaining beans, the tomatoes, stock and tomato purée. Season to taste with salt and pepper. Bring to the boil, then simmer for 10 minutes. Remove the pan from the heat, stir in the parsley and serve.

sausage and bean casserole

serves 4

1 tablespoon oil

1 onion, chopped

1 garlic clove, crushed

1 red pepper, cored, deseeded and chopped

4 lean pork sausages, quartered

2 x 410 g (13½ oz) cans mixed beans, drained and rinsed

400 g (13 oz) can chopped tomatoes

150 ml (¼ pint) vegetable stock

2 tablespoons tomato purée

2 tablespoons chopped parsley

salt and pepper

shepherd's pie

serves 4

2 tablespoons oil

500 g (1 lb) lean minced lamb

1 onion, finely chopped

2 carrots, finely chopped

2 celery sticks, finely chopped

1 garlic clove, finely chopped

1 tablespoon plain flour

300 ml (½ pint) chicken stock

2 tablespoons tomato purée

420 g (14 oz) can baked beans

1 kg (2 lb) floury potatoes. peeled and cut into pieces

50 g (2 oz) butter

milk, for mashed potatoes

salt and pepper

1 Heat the oil in a large, heavy-based saucepan and fry the lamb, stirring, until lightly browned. Add the vegetables and garlic and fry for a further 5 minutes.

2 Stir in the flour, stock, tomato purée and salt and pepper and heat until bubbling. Simmer gently for 30 minutes, adding a splash of water if the mixture starts to dry out. Stir in the baked beans and turn into a shallow ovenproof dish.

3 Meanwhile, cook the potatoes in plenty of lightly salted boiling water until tender. Drain and return to the pan. Mash well with the butter, milk and salt and pepper, making sure the mixture stays quite stiff.

4 Spoon the mashed potato over the meat mixture, spreading it in an even layer with a fork. Cook in a preheated oven, 190°C (375°F), Gas Mark 5, for 30–40 minutes until pale golden.

beef and bean stew *with cornmeal* dumplings

serves 6

375 g (12 oz) dried red or black
  kidney beans, soaked overnight

2 tablespoons olive oil

750 g (1½ lb) boneless shin of beef,
  cut into 2.5 cm (1 inch) cubes

1 large onion, chopped

2–3 garlic cloves, crushed

2 teaspoons ground cumin

2 teaspoons ground coriander

2–3 large red chillies, roasted, peeled,
  deseeded and finely chopped

2 red peppers, roasted, peeled,
  deseeded and finely chopped

1 bay leaf

1 thyme sprig

2 large tomatoes, about 300 g (10 oz),
  skinned and chopped

600 ml (1 pint) beef stock

about 300 ml (½ pint) water

6 tablespoons chopped coriander leaves

salt

for the cornmeal dumplings

65 g (2½ oz) plain flour

75 g (3 oz) fine cornmeal

1½ teaspoons caster sugar

1 teaspoon baking powder

¼ teaspoon salt

100 ml (3½ fl oz) buttermilk,
at room temperature

1 egg, beaten

25 g (1 oz) unsalted butter, melted

50 g (2 oz) canned sweetcorn
  kernels, drained

1 Drain the beans and rinse well. Put in a large saucepan of water and bring to the boil, then boil rapidly for 10 minutes. Drain and set aside.

2 Meanwhile, heat the oil in a large flameproof casserole, add the meat in batches and brown well all over. Remove the meat with a slotted spoon and set aside.

3 Add the onion and garlic to the casserole and cook until the onion is golden brown, then add the cumin and coriander and cook for 1–2 minutes.

4 Add the drained beans, the meat and all the remaining ingredients, except the coriander leaves and salt; the liquid should just cover the beef and vegetables. Bring to the boil, then cover tightly and simmer for 2–2½ hours until the meat is tender.

5 To make the dumplings, sift the flour, cornmeal, sugar, baking powder and salt into a bowl and mix together. Add the buttermilk, egg and butter and stir until combined, then gently stir in the sweetcorn.

6 Stir the coriander leaves into the stew and season with salt. Drop 12 spoonfuls of the dumpling mixture over the top of the stew, replace the lid and cook for a further 10–15 minutes until the dumplings are light and cooked.

saving energy

Trying to cut back and economize on your food budget isn't just about buying cheaper food and shopping more frugally. The energy you use to cook every day will have an impact on your fuel bills as well.

Slow-cooking savers

When you make slow-simmered dishes such as soups and stews, you'll use much more gas or electricity than you would for a quick-cook dish or if you were simply warming it up. Next time, make a double-batch in a large pan. That way you can pop half in the refrigerator or freezer for another day and will only be paying to re-heat the dish rather than cooking it from scratch. Good dishes to treat this way include soups, broths and stocks; stews and casseroles; curries; tomato and bolognese-style sauces.

Efficient baking and roasting

Don't put the oven on for just one dish. If you're going to bake or roast, cook other dishes at the same time so you're cooking all your dishes for the price of one.

For example, if you're roasting a chicken, roast or bake potatoes at the same time, and cook your veggies in the oven too. Carrots, parsnips, squash, onions and peppers all roast beautifully and make a sensational accompaniment to any baked or roasted meal.

Another way to fill that spare shelf in the oven is to make a dessert. Baked fruit, crumbles, tarts and pies can all be cooked while you're making the main meal – and they're good served both hot and warm, so if they've been sitting in a cooling oven while you've eaten your main course, no one will complain!

Microwave magic

Microwave ovens cook and warm food at a fraction of the time it would take to cook in an oven or on the hob. And although not all dishes are great cooked in a microwave, it's brilliant for many and will save on both time and energy. Great microwave savers include:

- steaming vegetables
- heating up dishes such as soups, stews and leftovers
- baking potatoes (start them off in the microwave until tender, then drizzle the skins with butter or olive oil and crisp them up in the oven)
- cooking steamed puddings such as Christmas pud or sticky toffee pudding
- making quick scrambled eggs or porridge
- melting ingredients such as chocolate and butter

Pressure cooker premiums

Using a pressure cooker may seem old-fashioned, but they're absolutely brilliant for reducing cooking times on slow-simmered dishes. Pulses, beans, soups, stews and casseroles can all be cooked in a fraction of the time using a pressure cooker, so if you cook lots of these kinds of dishes, invest in a pressure cooker and you really won't look back.

Get the right pans

Investing in good-quality pans will repay you in kind through their energy-efficient cooking. Look out for pans with heavy bases that retain heat and tight-fitting lids that hold in the heat, helping your food to cook more quickly and efficiently.

Steaming sensation

People love steaming vegetables and other foods because it's such a healthy, gentle, delicious way to cook, but steaming foods offers the opportunity for saving energy too. Buy a layered steamer with stacking levels so that you can do all your steaming on one ring.

Kettle cunning

When you need to boil the kettle, think about how much water you really need. If it's just for one cup of tea, then don't fill the kettle up, or even halfway. There's no point in using the energy to boil up a whole kettleful if you only need a small amount – so always check how much water is in the kettle, how much you need and then heat just enough water. Also, think about using the kettle to heat up water you want to cook in, such as for a pan of pasta or some frozen peas. Bringing the water to the boil will be quicker in a kettle than in the pan itself, so saving energy. Again, heat only a small amount if it's to fill only a small saucepan.

Saving water

Water is an important resource, too, so re-think how you splash out in the kitchen:

•

Wash fruit and veg in a bowl rather than under running water.

•

A modern dishwasher typically uses less water than hand-washing and rinsing the same number of dirty dishes in the sink.

•

Keep a bottle of water in the refrigerator so you can enjoy cold water instantly rather than running a tap until it's cold.

•

If your tap's dripping, fix that washer.

serves 4

250 g (8 oz) basmati rice

100 g (3½ oz) frozen baby broad beans

4 eggs

25 g (1 oz) butter

1 small onion, finely chopped

1 teaspoon medium curry paste

400 g (13 oz) can tuna in oil or brine, drained and flaked into chunks

small handful of flat leaf parsley, chopped

salt and pepper

to garnish

flat leaf parsley sprigs

lemon or lime wedges

tuna kedgeree

1 Cook the rice in plenty of lightly salted boiling water for about 8 minutes until almost tender. Add the broad beans, return to the boil and cook for a further 3 minutes, then drain.

2 Meanwhile, boil the eggs in a pan of water for 8 minutes, then cool in cold water. Shell the eggs and cut lengthways into quarters.

3 Melt the butter in a large frying pan, add the onion and curry paste and fry gently for 3 minutes. Add the drained rice, broad beans, tuna and eggs.

4 Stir in the parsley and season the kedgeree with salt and pepper to taste. Stir gently over a low heat for 1 minute, then transfer to serving plates. Garnish with parsley and lemon or lime wedges.

fish pie

serves 6

1 Put the fish, bay leaf, onion and peppercorns in a large pan with enough milk to cover. Bring to the boil, then simmer gently until the fish is cooked. Strain the fish liquid into a measuring jug and make it up to 450 ml (¾ pint) with more milk or some water, if necessary.

2 Melt the butter in a heavy-based saucepan, stir in the flour and cook over a low heat for 1 minute. Remove the pan from the heat and gradually add the fish liquid, stirring constantly. Once all the liquid has been incorporated, return the pan to a low heat and bring to the boil, stirring constantly until the sauce is smooth and thick. Leave to simmer for a few minutes, then season to taste with salt and pepper and stir in the parsley or dill.

3 Meanwhile, boil the potatoes in a large saucepan of lightly salted boiling water for 10 minutes until tender. Drain, beat to a purée with the hot milk and season to taste with salt and pepper.

4 Pour a little of the sauce into a greased ovenproof dish and lay the fish on top of it. Top with the tomato slices and cover with the remaining sauce, then pile the puréed potato on top. Brown under a preheated hot grill for a few minutes before serving.

750 g (1½ lb) cod or haddock fillets, or a mixture of white fish

1 bay leaf

½ onion, sliced

6 peppercorns

about 300 ml (1 pint) milk

25 g (1 oz) butter

3 tablespoons plain flour

2 tablespoons chopped parsley or dill

1 kg (2 lb) potatoes, peeled and cut into pieces

150 ml (¼ pint) hot milk

4 tomatoes, skinned and sliced

salt and white pepper

fish and chips

serves 4

125 g (4 oz) self-raising flour, plus extra for dusting

½ teaspoon baking powder

¼ teaspoon turmeric

200 ml (7 fl oz) water

1.5 kg (3 lb) large potatoes, peeled

750 g (1½ lb) piece of skinless cod or haddock fillet

sunflower oil or groundnut oil, for deep-frying

salt and pepper

cooked peas, to serve

1 Mix together the flour, baking powder, turmeric and
a pinch of salt in a mixing bowl and make a well in
the centre. Pour one-half of the water into the well,
gradually whisking it into the flour to make a smooth
batter, then whisk in the remainder.

2 Cut the potatoes into 1.5 cm (¾ inch) slices, then cut
across to make chunky chips. Put them in a bowl
of cold water.

3 Check the fish for any stray bones and pat dry on kitchen
paper, then cut into 4 portions. Season lightly and dust
with flour. Drain the chips thoroughly and pat dry on
kitchen paper.

4 In a large, heavy-based saucepan or wok, heat sufficient
oil for deep-frying to 180–190°C (350–375°F), or until a
cube of bread browns in 30 seconds. Fry one-half of the
chips for 10 minutes, or until golden. Drain and keep
warm while you cook the remainder, then remove the
second batch and keep that warm too.

5 Dip 2 of the fish pieces in the batter and lower them
into the hot oil. Fry gently for 4–5 minutes, or until crisp
and golden. Drain and keep warm while you fry the
remaining pieces. Serve the fish and chips with the peas.

vegetable moussaka

serves 4

50 g (2 oz) butter

3 tablespoons vegetable oil

2 aubergines, thinly sliced

4 potatoes, peeled and thinly sliced

3 large onions, chopped

2 garlic cloves, chopped

3 large tomatoes, skinned and sliced

salt and pepper

for the cheese sauce

50 g (2 oz) butter

40 g (1½ oz) wholemeal flour

600 ml (1 pint) milk

250 g (8 oz) Cheddar cheese, grated

½–1 teaspoon grated nutmeg

1 teaspoon French mustard

1 Heat one-half of the butter and one-half of the oil in a frying pan, add the aubergines and potatoes in batches and cook for 10 minutes, turning once. Remove from the pan.

2 Heat the rest of the butter and oil, add the onions, garlic and tomatoes and cook for 10 minutes, making sure they do not brown. Mix one-half of the aubergine and potato slices with the onion mixture and season to taste. Reserve the rest of the aubergine and potato slices for the topping.

3 To make the sauce, melt the butter in a heavy-based saucepan, stir in the flour and cook over a low heat for 1 minute. Remove the pan from the heat and gradually add the milk, stirring constantly. Once all the milk has been incorporated, return the pan to a low heat and bring to the boil, stirring constantly until the sauce is smooth and thick. Leave to simmer for a few minutes, then add about 175 g (6 oz) of the Cheddar, the nutmeg and mustard and season to taste with salt and pepper.

4 Spoon one-half of the mixed vegetables into a casserole and cover with one-half of the sauce, then add the remaining vegetables. Top with a neat layer of aubergine and potato slices and cover with the remaining sauce.

5 Cover the casserole with a lid and bake in a preheated oven, 160°C (325°F), Gas Mark 3, for 1¼ hours. Remove the lid and add the remaining Cheddar, then return the dish to the oven, raising the heat slightly, and cook for a further 10 minutes, or until the cheese topping has melted.

1 Slice the pumpkin in half across its widest part and discard the seeds and fibres. Cut the flesh into cubes, removing the skin. You should have about 1 kg (2 lb) flesh.

2 Heat the oil in a large saucepan and fry the onion, garlic and chilli until soft but not coloured. Add the pumpkin and celery and fry gently for 10 minutes. Stir in the carrots, parsnips, tomatoes, tomato pureé, paprika, stock and bouquet garni. Bring to the boil, then cover and simmer for 1–1½ hours, until the vegetables are tender.

3 Add the kidney beans and cook for a further 10 minutes, then season with salt and pepper. Garnish with parsley and serve with crusty bread or mashed potatoes.

serves 8–10

1 pumpkin, about 1.5 kg (3 lb)

4 tablespoons sunflower or olive oil

1 large onion, finely chopped

3–4 garlic cloves, crushed

1 small red chilli, deseeded and chopped

4 celery sticks, cut into 2.5 cm (1 inch) lengths

6–8 carrots, cut into 2.5 cm (1 inch) chunks

175 g (6 oz) parsnips, cut into 2.5 cm (1 inch) chunks

2 x 400 g (13 oz) cans plum tomatoes

3 tablespoons tomato purée

1–2 tablespoons hot paprika

125–250 ml (4–8 fl oz) vegetable stock

1 bouquet garni

2 x 410 g (13½ oz) cans red kidney beans, drained and rinsed

salt and pepper

3–4 tablespoons finely chopped parsley, to garnish

crusty bread or mashed potatoes, to serve

pumpkin
and root vegetable
stew

sweet
things

serves 4

for the pancakes
2 bananas
1 teaspoon vanilla extract
150 g (5 oz) self-raising flour
1 teaspoon baking powder
1 tablespoon caster sugar
1 egg
75 ml (3 fl oz) milk
15 g (½ oz) unsalted butter, melted
sunflower oil, for frying

vanilla and banana
pancakes
with maple syrup butter

for the maple syrup butter
125 g (4 oz) unsalted butter, softened
2 tablespoons maple syrup
1 tablespoon icing sugar, sifted
a few drops vanilla extract (optional)

1 To make the maple syrup butter, put the butter in a bowl and gradually beat in the maple syrup and icing sugar, together with the vanilla extract, if using. Cover and chill while you make the pancakes.

2 Mash the bananas with the vanilla extract in a bowl to make a smooth purée. Sift the flour and baking powder into a separate bowl and stir in the sugar.

3 Beat the egg, milk and melted butter together in another bowl, then beat into the dry ingredients until smooth. Stir in the banana purée.

4 Heat a little oil in a large frying pan or griddle pan over a medium heat. Drop 4 tablespoonfuls of the batter, well spaced apart, into the pan and cook for 2 minutes, or until bubbles form on the surfaces and the undersides are golden brown. Using a spatula, turn the pancakes over and cook on the other side for 1–2 minutes. Remove from the pan, wrap in a tea towel and keep warm while cooking the remaining batter in the same way, making 12 small pancakes in all.

5 Transfer the pancakes to a serving plate and serve with the maple syrup butter.

feeding (and filling) *kids*

When it comes to keeping your family full, most parents know that they've got their work cut out. Growing bodies are busy all the time and seem to need constant feeding – and for parents of picky eaters the job is even harder. But how do you keep your kids full and fit, and still stick to your budget?

Energy food

The great news is that loads of the foods that give your kids bags of energy are cheap and healthy. We're talking about carbohydrates here – pasta, potatoes, rice, beans and wholegrain breads. They're all packed with essential carbohydrates that convert directly into the energy your kids use up to grow and run around. So pile on the potatoes and pasta, then think about the other essential food groups your kids need to stay strong, fit and healthy.

Protein

Essential for growth and repair of cells, protein can be found in meat, poultry, fish, pulses and beans, tofu, eggs and dairy foods. Keep protein choices varied so that your kids benefit from all the extra nutrients that different protein foods offer. These foods can be pricey but there are still plenty of ways to ensure your kids get the protein they need without spending a fortune:

• Canned fish are often better value than fresh and are great on baked potatoes, in pasta sauces, on toast and in many other dishes.
• Good-quality, low-fat mince for burgers, meatballs, bolognese, lasagne and shepherd's pie is a popular, economical source of red meat.
• Chicken portions are more affordable than chicken breasts or fillets – and healthy too if you remove the skin and trim off any excess fat – so try them in casseroles or marinate and grill or bake.
• Vegetarian choices such as beans, pulses, lentils and eggs are cheaper than meat alternatives.

Dairy foods

Packed with calcium for healthy bones and teeth, these include milk, cheese and yogurt. (Non-dairy foods such as soya beans, tofu, nuts and canned fish with soft, edible bones such as sardines are also rich in calcium.) Make common-sense savings:

• Buy large tubs of yogurt rather than individual tubs and spoon a serving into a small bowl.
• Buy economical large cartons of milk rather than several smaller ones (but only if you know you'll use them up in time).
• Dried soya beans are cheaper than canned, but make sure you have time for soaking and boiling.
• Tofu varies in taste and texture according to the type and brand you buy. Shop around until you find a brand or variety your kids like.

Fruit and veg

Packed with healthy nutrients and fibre, plenty of fruit and veg should be eaten regularly by kids. But what about the price? Just follow the tips on shopping (see pages 164–5) and eating seasonally (see pages 212–13) and you won't go far wrong.

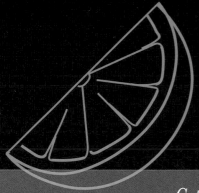

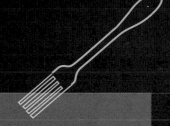

Coping with picky eaters

If you find yourself endlessly throwing good food away because your kids have decided they don't like it or don't fancy it – don't despair!

•

Create temptation
Sometimes a bit of extra preparation is all you need. Cut carrot and cucumber into bite-sized sticks and serve with a bowl of creamy yogurt dip, or cut whole fruits such as apples and pears into appealing wedges.

•

Let your kids choose
Ask your kids to help you write the shopping list, choosing healthy ingredients they like, and then encourage them to try something new as well. This technique can help to broaden their repertoire – giving you more flexibility with your shopping and budget.

•

Try it a different way
Sometimes the problem isn't the ingredient itself but the way it's cooked. If the kids don't like something cooked one way – try it another and you may find it a success.

Veggie avoiders
If your kids refuse to eat their greens, the only answer is to hide them! Blended soups are the perfect place because once you've whizzed them up, there won't be a vegetable in sight. Sauces and stews are other good hiding places – just chop them up extra-fine and they'll virtually disappear – or mash other root veg in with their potatoes

•

Get fruity
If your kids are funny about fruit, try puréeing soft or poached fruits and stirring into yogurt or spooning over ice cream. This works for fresh, frozen and canned – so when favourite fruits are out of season, you can still get your kids eating affordable fruit.

pancake stack with
summer fruits

1 Put the fruit in a bowl and sift the icing sugar over. Turn and stir the fruit gently a few times to encourage the juices to run, then set aside.

2 Put all the pancake ingredients in a food processor or liquidizer and blend until smooth and creamy, or whisk in a mixing bowl.

3 Heat a little oil in a large frying pan or griddle pan over a medium heat. Drop 4 tablespoonfuls of the batter, well spaced apart, in the pan and cook for 2 minutes, or until bubbles form on the surfaces and the undersides are golden brown. Using a spatula, turn the pancakes over and cook on the other side for 1–2 minutes. Remove from the pan, wrap in a tea towel and keep warm while cooking the remaining batter in the same way, making 12 small pancakes in all.

4 Stir the fruit gently a few more times, then serve the pancakes, 3 per person, topped with the fruit mixture and with 2 scoops of ice cream.

serves 4

125 g (4 oz) strawberries, halved or quartered, if large

125 g (4 oz) raspberries

125 g (4 oz) blueberries

25 g (1 oz) icing sugar

8 scoops of vanilla ice cream, to serve

for the pancakes

75 g (3 oz) plain flour

1 egg

125 ml (4 fl oz) milk

2½ tablespoons sunflower oil, plus extra for frying

1 tablespoon caster sugar

serves 4

1 kg (2 lb) Bramley apples, peeled, cored and thickly sliced

25 g (1 oz) butter

2 tablespoons caster sugar

1 tablespoon lemon juice

2 tablespoons water

cream or ice cream, to serve

for the crumble

50 g (2 oz) butter

75 g (3 oz) fresh wholemeal breadcrumbs

25 g (1 oz) pumpkin seeds

2 tablespoons soft light brown sugar

1 Place the apples in a saucepan with the butter, sugar, lemon juice and water. Bring to the boil, then cover and simmer for 8–10 minutes until softened.

2 Melt the butter for the crumble in a frying pan and stir-fry the breadcrumbs until lightly golden. Add the pumpkin seeds and stir-fry for a further 1 minute, then remove from the heat and stir in the sugar.

3 Spoon the apple mixture into bowls, sprinkle the crumble over the top and serve with cream or ice cream.

instant
apple crumbles

banoffi pie

serves 6–8

for the crumb case
125 g (4 oz) butter
250 g (8 oz) digestive biscuits, crushed

for the filling
175 g (6 oz) butter
175 g (6 oz) caster sugar
425 g (14 oz) can condensed milk
2 bananas
1 tablespoon lemon juice
150 ml (¼ pint) whipping cream
25 g (1 oz) plain dark chocolate,
    grated

1 To make the crumb case, melt the butter in a saucepan and stir in the biscuit crumbs. Press the mixture evenly over the base and sides of a deep 20 cm (8 inch) loose-bottomed flan tin. Chill until firm.

2 To make the filling, put the butter and sugar in a saucepan and heat gently, stirring, until the butter has melted, then stir in the condensed milk. Bring to the boil, then simmer for 5 minutes, stirring occasionally, until the mixture becomes a caramel colour. Pour into the base and leave to cool, then chill until set.

3 Slice the bananas and toss them in the lemon juice. Reserve one-quarter of the banana slices for decoration and spread the rest over the filling. Whip the cream until it forms soft peaks and spread it over the top. Decorate with the reserved banana slices and sprinkle with chocolate.

blackberry *muffin* *slice*

serves 6—8

100 g (3½ oz) unsalted butter, plus extra for greasing

250 g (8 oz) plain flour

2 teaspoons baking powder

150 g (5 oz) caster sugar, plus extra for sprinkling

25 g (1 oz) porridge oats

100 g (3½ oz) fresh blackberries

175 ml (6 fl oz) milk

1 egg, beaten

1 Grease and line the base and sides of a 500 g (1 lb) loaf tin so that the greaseproof paper comes about 1 cm (½ inch) above the rim of the tin, then grease the paper.

2 Sift the flour and baking powder into a mixing bowl, add the sugar, oats and one-half of the blackberries and mix well.

3 Melt the butter in a saucepan and stir in the milk and egg. Pour this mixture into the bowl and stir into the dry ingredients until just combined but still a bit lumpy. Turn the mixture into the tin and scatter with the remaining blackberries.

4 Bake in a preheated oven, 180°C (350°F), Gas Mark 4, for 50–60 minutes, or until well risen, golden and firm to the touch.

5 Leave in the tin for 5 minutes, then transfer to a wire rack and sprinkle with a little extra sugar. Serve warm or cold.

chocolate
refrigerator cake

1 Line a dampened 500 g (1 lb) loaf tin with clingfilm. Put the chocolate and butter in a bowl over a pan of simmering water and leave to melt, stirring frequently. Remove from the heat and leave to cool a little.

2 Stir the biscuits, nuts and caramel bar pieces into the melted mixture until combined, then turn the mixture into the tin and pack down in an even layer. Chill for several hours, or overnight, until set.

3 Invert the cake on to a plate and remove the tin. Leave the cake to soften a little at room temperature, then peel away the clingfilm and cut into small slices.

serves 10

300 g (10 oz) plain dark chocolate, broken into pieces

75 g (3 oz) unsalted butter

125 g (4 oz) shortbread biscuits, broken into small pieces

125 g (4 oz) whole mixed nuts, such as almonds, hazelnuts and Brazil nuts

150 g (5 oz) milk chocolate caramel bar, broken into sections

cinnamon doughnuts

makes 12

100 ml (3½ fl oz) hand-hot water

2 teaspoons dried active yeast

175 g (6 oz) caster sugar

400 g (13 oz) strong white bread flour,
plus extra for dusting

1 egg, beaten

50 g (2 oz) lightly salted butter, melted

100 ml (3½ fl oz) hand-hot milk

vegetable oil, for oiling

½ teaspoon ground cinnamon

vegetable oil, for deep-frying

1 Place the water in a small bowl, stir in the yeast
  and 1 teaspoon of the sugar and leave to stand for
  10 minutes, or until frothy. Mix the flour with 75 g
  (3 oz) of the sugar in a large mixing bowl. Add the egg,
  butter, milk and yeasted mixture and mix to a dough.

2 On a lightly floured surface, knead gently for 10 minutes,
  or until smooth and elastic. Put into a lightly oiled bowl,
  cover with clingfilm and leave in a warm place for about
  1 hour, or until doubled in size.

3 Tip the dough on to a lightly floured surface and punch
  it a few times to knock the air out of it, then knead
  lightly to form into a ball. Divide into 12 equal pieces
  and roll each one into a ball. Place the balls on 2 lightly
  oiled baking sheets, spaced well apart to allow for
  rising, and cover loosely with oiled clingfilm. Leave to
  rise for about 40 minutes, or until doubled in size.

4 Mix the cinnamon on a plate with the remaining sugar.
  In a large, heavy-based saucepan or wok, heat sufficient
  oil for deep-frying to 180–190°C (350–375°F), or until a
  cube of bread browns in 30 seconds. Fry the doughnuts,
  a few at a time, for 2–3 minutes, or until puffed up and
  golden. Drain with a slotted spoon and place on
  kitchen paper, then toss in the cinnamon sugar and
  serve immediately.

edible gifts

When it comes to birthdays, Christmas and all those other times for giving, the cost can soon add up – often unnecessarily. So why not return to that old-fashioned tradition of making edible gifts? It's absolutely true that it's the effort that counts, and you'll be thrilled to see the look of joy on someone's face when they open up a box of freshly made cookies or some homemade sweets that you've made especially for them. Edible gifts can be ideal for any occasion, whether it's a small something such as a jar of homemade jam to say thank you, an extravagant hamper for your dad's birthday, a cake for Mother's Day or some homemade sweets as a hostess gift. Check out the ideas below for inspiration, then get cooking!

Sweet ideas

Everyone loves cakes and sweets, and because they're something of an indulgent treat, it makes them perfect for giving. Great sweet gifts include cupcakes and larger cakes; cookies and sweet biscuits; toffee, fudge and other sweets; chocolate-dipped fruit such as cherries and strawberries; petits fours.

Savoury somethings

For those with less of a sweet tooth, there are all kinds of savoury goodies you can package up as a gift, such as savoury crackers and biscuits; potted meats, shellfish or fish; pâtés and pastes; as well as chutneys and relishes, which make the perfect companions to many of the above.

Perfect preserves

Homemade preserves are the ideal gift, and great for Christmas-time when you find yourself in need of a supply of small gifts. Save pretty jars during the year in preparation, then cook up a large batch of your favourite preserve, add a decorative label (including the date it was made), then sit back and relax. Great preserves include jams and jellies; fruit curds, butters and cheeses; marmalades; bottled fruits; pickles, chutneys and relishes.

The art of presentation

It's often the presentation that transforms a tasty homemade treat into a special gift. Try out some of the ideas below to wow friends and family, and enjoy delighting them without spending a fortune.

- For a simple cake on a plate, take time to decorate the cake beautifully and tie a ribbon around it.
- Look out for decorative tins or jars to package cookies, cakes, savoury crackers and other foods that need to be stored in an airtight containers.
- Pack small sweets, cookies and petits fours into glass jars and top the lid with pretty paper or fabric tied with a ribbon.
- Make pretty labels for your homemade treats.
- Buy pretty boxes from stationers to hold the goodies, or create your own by covering a cardboard box with pretty wrapping paper.
- Nestle jars or containers inside your presentation box with coloured tissue paper.
- Add pretty ribbons and gift tags as the finishing touch to your gift.

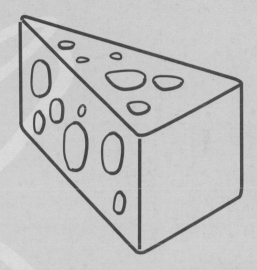

Gorgeous hampers and food boxes

For the ultimate in presentation, how about making a hamper or food box? If you're not entirely confident in the kitchen, you can always buy lots of your edible gifts, or make some yourself and supplement them with goodies from the supermarket. Find a wicker hamper or pretty box and pad the base with tissue paper before filling with edible treats and tying it up with a big bow. Think about who the hamper is for and the kinds of food they like, then tailor the contents accordingly. Here are some ideas to get you going.

- **Deli delights** Buy a few gourmet cheeses and supplement them with savoury crackers, chutneys and potted meats or pâtés.
- **Sweet selection** Make or buy a variety of cookies, cakes, sweet preserves and candy.
- **Savoury somethings** Choose spiced nuts, marinated olives, flavoured vinegar and extra virgin olive oil.
- **Fresh and healthy** Fresh fruit and gourmet vegetables can be a real luxury, so why not fill up a hamper with delicious fresh produce for someone who loves fresh food and cooking?
- **Afternoon tea** Pack freshly baked scones, homemade jam and luxury tea leaves for a birthday indulgence.
- **Morning coffee** Dark chocolate brownies and fresh coffee grounds will lift anyone's day.

Food safety

Don't forget that many foods need to be stored in airtight containers or in the refrigerator, so store all food gifts correctly and pack up or wrap just before giving to ensure they're safe to eat. Make sure the recipient knows which items, if any, need to be stored in the refrigerator.

•

Many people suffer from allergies, so if your gift contains common allergens such as nuts, dairy, wheat or gluten, eggs, yeast or soya, be sure to label the gift with its ingredients so that the person you give it to can not only enjoy it him or herself but can also share it with others.

makes 20

125 g (4 oz) unsalted butter, softened, plus extra for greasing

100 g (3½ oz) golden caster sugar

225 g (7½ oz) self-raising flour, sifted

1 teaspoon ground ginger

1 teaspoon ground cinnamon

1 egg, beaten

150 ml (¼ pint) milk

100 g (3½ oz) sultanas

75 g (3 oz) currants

50 g (2 oz) white sugar cubes

1 Grease 2 baking sheets. Put the butter and sugar in a mixing bowl and beat until light and fluffy. Stir in the flour, spices, egg and milk and mix to form a soft dough, then stir in the dried fruit.

2 Place dessertspoonfuls of the mixture on to the baking sheets, spacing them slightly apart.

3 Put the sugar cubes in a polythene bag and lightly crush with a rolling pin, then scatter the sugar over the buns. Bake in a preheated oven, 190°C (375°F), Gas Mark 5, for about 15 minutes, or until risen and golden. Transfer to a wire rack to cool.

rock buns

crumbly raspberry and oat slices

makes 12–14

175 g (6 oz) butter, slightly softened and diced, plus extra for greasing

100 g (3½ oz) plain flour

75 g (3 oz) plain wholemeal flour

175 g (6 oz) porridge oats

150 g (5 oz) golden caster sugar

finely grated rind of 1 lemon

250 g (8 oz) fresh or frozen raspberries

icing sugar, sifted, for dusting

1 Lightly grease the base and sides of a shallow 27 x 18 cm (10½ x 7 inch) baking tin or a similar-sized roasting tin.

2 Put the flours, oats and butter in a large mixing bowl and work with your fingers until the mixture forms a coarse crumble. Stir in the sugar and lemon rind and continue to work the mixture until it starts to cling together.

3 Turn one-half of the mixture into the tin and pat it down into an even layer. Scatter the raspberries on top and sprinkle the remaining crumble mixture over them.

4 Bake in a preheated oven, 180°C (350°F), Gas Mark 4, for about 1 hour or until the topping begins to turn golden. Cut into fingers and leave to cool in the tin. Serve dusted with icing sugar.

impress
for less

celebrating in style

Shopping and cooking on a budget is one thing when you're dealing with everyday family meals, but what about when you want to celebrate a birthday, have friends around for a meal or just spoil your partner? Well, the good news is that with a bit of creative thinking, intelligent planning and crafty shopping you can cook meals that will most definitely impress without costing you a fortune. The simplest and often cheapest ingredients, cooked with flair, can be just as impressive as haute cuisine dishes, and you can easily create a great atmosphere by setting the table beautifully, using candles to create a magical effect and serving food in individual dishes for a sophisticated touch.

starters

pork patties
with
soured cream and dill sauce

serves 4

500 g (1 lb) lean minced pork

40 g (1½ oz) fresh white breadcrumbs

1 small onion, grated

1 teaspoon paprika

1 egg, beaten

8 slices of pancetta or thin rashers of smoked streaky bacon

25 g (1 oz) butter

1 tablespoon vegetable oil

150 ml (¼ pint) soured cream

2 tablespoons chopped dill

2 teaspoons pink or green peppercorns, lightly crushed

salt and pepper

1 Put the pork, breadcrumbs, onion, paprika, egg and a little salt and pepper in a bowl and mix until evenly combined. This is most easily done with your hands.

2 Divide the mixture into 8 equal pieces and shape them into patties. Wrap a slice of pancetta or bacon around each one, securing it with a wooden cocktail stick.

3 Melt the butter with the oil in a large, heavy-based frying pan and gently fry the patties for 5 minutes on each side until golden. Drain and transfer to serving plates.

4 Add the soured cream, dill and peppercorns to the pan and heat gently, stirring, until smooth and creamy. Season to taste and serve with the patties.

serves 4

2 garlic cloves, crushed

grated rind and juice of 1 lemon

4 thyme sprigs, leaves only

6 tablespoons extra virgin olive oil

1 tablespoon clear honey

1 teaspoon dried oregano

1 teaspoon ground cumin

12 chicken wings

salt and pepper

lemon and herb chicken wings

1 Place the garlic, lemon rind and juice in a medium bowl. Add the thyme leaves, oil, honey, oregano and cumin and season to taste with salt and pepper.

2 Add the chicken wings and stir until they are well coated with the marinade.

3 Cook the chicken wings under a preheated medium-hot grill for 15–20 minutes, turning and basting until charred and cooked through.

spicy maple
ribs

serves 4

meaty spare ribs

salt

lemon or lime wedges, to garnish

for the marinade

100 ml (3½ fl oz) maple syrup

2 garlic cloves, crushed

3 tablespoons white wine vinegar

3 tablespoons tomato purée

finely grated rind and juice
  of 1 lemon

1 red chilli, deseeded and
  finely chopped

½ teaspoon smoked paprika

1 Arrange the spare ribs in a single layer in a shallow, non-metallic dish. Put all the marinade ingredients in a bowl and beat together, then pour the mixture over the ribs, turning them until they are completely coated. Cover and leave to marinate in the refrigerator for at least 4 hours and up to 24 hours.

2 Transfer the ribs to a shallow roasting tin, pour the excess marinade from the dish over them and season lightly with salt.

3 Bake in a preheated oven, 180°C (350°F), Gas Mark 4, for 1½–1¾ hours, basting occasionally with the juices, until the meat is tender and the juices are thick and sticky. Garnish with lemon or lime wedges.

Potted prawns
with fennel pittas

serves 4

200 g (7 oz) butter
1 small head of fennel, finely chopped
1 teaspoon finely grated lemon rind
1 teaspoon fennel seeds, crushed
4 small round pitta breads
350 g (11½ oz) raw peeled prawns
1 garlic clove, crushed
good pinch of paprika
¼ teaspoon ground mace
salt and pepper

1 Melt 15 g (½ oz) of the butter in a frying pan and fry the fennel gently for 5 minutes, or until soft. Stir in the lemon rind and fennel seeds and season with salt and pepper. Split the pittas down one side and spread the fennel mixture inside. Flatten them firmly under the palms of your hands.

2 Melt another 25 g (1 oz) of the butter in a large frying pan and gently fry the prawns for about 2 minutes, in batches if necessary, turning once, or until they are deep pink on both sides. When all the prawns are cooked, stir in the garlic, paprika and mace.

3 Pack the prawns into 4 x 125 ml (4 fl oz) ramekins or shallow dishes. Melt the remaining butter in a small saucepan, skimming off any foam from the surface, and spoon over the prawns so that they are mostly submerged. Cover and chill for 2 hours, or until the butter has set.

4 Heat a ridged grill pan or grill and lightly toast the pittas on both sides. Cut into fingers and serve with the prawns.

budget *menus*

You can know the theory about watching your pennies and getting the most out of your shopping, but sometimes putting it into practice can be a little bit harder. To make your job easier, we've done some of the thinking for you, using the recipes in this book to make amazing meals for less.

Everyday menus

Trying to plan your menu for the week ahead? Take a look at some of the ideas below and find inspiration to help you on your way. We've provided ideas for the main meals, but don't forget to think about snacks too.

Sunday
Breakfast cereal with milk and fruit
Lunch Stuffed Pot-roast Chicken (page 146), Roast Potatoes with Rosemary and Garlic (page 136), Roast Vegetables with Olive Oil and Chillies (page 140), Spicy Stir-fried Cauliflower with Almonds (page 142) and steamed green veg; for pudding: Pears with Chocolate Crumble (page 179)
Supper Boston Baked Beans (page 74) on toast

Monday
Breakfast porridge with dried fruit
Lunch chicken salad sandwiches (made using the leftover roast chicken from Sunday lunch)
Dinner bubble and squeak with poached eggs (made using up leftover roast potatoes and greens from Sunday lunch)

Tuesday
Breakfast muesli with yogurt and fruit
Lunch vegetable soup (made with leftover vegetables from Sunday lunch) with a crusty roll and some cheese
Dinner Chilli con Carne (page 206) served with rice, chopped avocado, natural yogurt and chopped tomatoes

Wednesday
Breakfast boiled egg with toast
Lunch Minestrone Soup (page 60) with a crusty roll
Dinner Sausage and Bean Casserole (page 86)

Thursday
Breakfast cereal with milk and fruit
Lunch Spanish Omelette (page 67) with salad
Dinner Ham and Egg Linguini (page 84) with a side salad

Friday
Breakfast muesli with yogurt and fruit
Lunch Quiche Lorraine (page 66), with salad
Dinner Fish with Sweet Potato and Spinach Mash (page 163)

Saturday
Breakfast Vanilla and Banana Pancakes with Maple Syrup Butter (page 100)
Lunch Carrot and Lentil Soup (page 63) with a crusty roll
Dinner Garlic, Herb and Bean Pâté (page 128), then Chicken and Lemon Paella (page 82), served with a side salad, followed by ice cream and fruit

Dinner parties with dash

Entertaining can take all shapes and forms, whether it's an elegant evening meal to impress, fun with friends, or splashing out for the family. Try one of these fab menus for no-fuss entertaining on a budget.

Feeding friends
Starter Lemon and Herb Chicken Wings (page 122)
Main course Butternut Squash Risotto (page 196)
Dessert Instant Apple Crumbles (page 105)

Elegant entertaining
Starter Potted Prawns with Fennel Pittas (page 124)
Main course Cherry Tomato Tarts with Pesto (page 166) served with Rösti (page 134) and green salad
Dessert Banoffi Pie (page 106)

Family lunch
Starter Bright Red Pepper Soup (page 62)
Main course Fish Pie (page 93) with peas
Dessert Lemon and Bay Custards (page 175)

Romantic dinner for two

Spoiling your partner can be difficult when you're on a limited budget, but the ideas below are certain to bring a little love back into your life. Making the effort to make a delicious meal is certain to enchant your amour.

The perfect date
Starter Pork Patties with Sour Cream and Dill (page 120)
Main course Venetian-style Calves' Liver (page 153)
Dessert Red Berry Terrine (page 178)

For that special occasion
Starter Tomato and Green Bean Salad (page 144)
Main course Braised Fish with Lentils (page 156)
Dessert Lavender Crême Brûlées (page 172)

Romantic evening in
Starter Tomato Bruschetta (page 187)
Lunch Spaghetti Carbonara (page 195)
Dinner Chocolate Risotto (page 174)

garlic, herb and bean pâté

serves 2

410 g (13½ oz) can flageolet beans, drained and rinsed

125 g (4 oz) cream cheese

2 garlic cloves, chopped

3 tablespoons ready-made pesto

2 spring onions, chopped

salt and pepper

chopped flat leaf parsley, to garnish (optional)

to serve

25 g (1 oz) rocket leaves

16 radishes

8 crisp breads

1 Place the beans, cream cheese, garlic and pesto in a food processor or liquidizer and blend until combined. Add the spring onions and salt and pepper and process for 10 seconds.

2 Turn the mixture into a serving dish and chill until ready to serve. Scatter with chopped parsley, if liked, and serve with the rocket leaves, radishes and crisp breads.

green lentil soup
with *spiced butter*

1 Heat the oil in a saucepan, add the onions and sauté for 3 minutes, then add the bay leaves, lentils, stock and turmeric. Bring to the boil, then cover and simmer for 20 minutes, or until the lentils are tender and turning mushy.

2 Meanwhile, put all the spiced butter ingredients in a bowl and beat together, then transfer the butter to a small serving dish.

3 When the lentils are cooked, stir the coriander leaves into the soup and season to taste with salt and pepper.

4 Ladle into warm soup bowls and serve with the spiced butter for stirring into the soup.

serves 4

2 tablespoons olive oil

2 onions, chopped

2 bay leaves

175 g (6 oz) green lentils, rinsed

1 litre (1¾ pints) vegetable stock

½ teaspoon turmeric

small handful of coriander leaves, roughly chopped

salt and pepper

for the spiced butter

50 g (2 oz) lightly salted butter, softened

1 large garlic clove, crushed

1 tablespoon chopped coriander

1 teaspoon paprika

1 teaspoon cumin seeds

1 red chilli, deseeded and finely chopped

serves 6

4 carrots, chopped

2 parsnips, chopped

1 tablespoon olive oil

1 leek, trimmed, cleaned and
  finely chopped

1.2 litres (2 pints) vegetable stock

2 teaspoons thyme leaves

salt and pepper

thyme sprigs, to garnish

1 Place the carrots and parsnips in a roasting tin, drizzle with the oil and toss to coat, then season with salt and pepper. Roast in a preheated oven, 200°C (400°F), Gas Mark 6, for 1 hour or until the vegetables are very soft.

2 Meanwhile, 20 minutes before the root vegetables will be cooked, put the leek in a large saucepan with the stock and 1 teaspoon of the thyme. Bring to the boil, then cover and simmer for 20 minutes.

3 Transfer the roasted root vegetables to a food processor or liquidizer and blend, adding a little of the stock from the pan if necessary. Alternatively, rub through a fine sieve. Add to the leeks with the remaining thyme and season to taste. Bring to the boil, then stir and simmer for 5 minutes.

4 Ladle into warm soup bowls and garnish with the thyme sprigs.

root vegetable soup

sides

scalloped
potatoes

serves 4

vegetable oil, for greasing

75 ml (3 fl oz) soured cream

350 ml (12 fl oz) milk

25 g (1 oz) butter

1 tablespoon cornflour

4 potatoes, about 750 g (1½ lb),
  peeled and cut into 5 mm
  (¼ inch) slices

½ onion, chopped

pepper

to garnish
pinch of paprika

thyme sprigs

1 Brush a 20 x 12 cm (8 x 5 inch) baking dish with oil.

2 Put the soured cream, milk, butter, cornflour and some pepper in a bowl and whisk together.

3 Place one-third of the potato slices in the bottom of the dish, pour one-third of the soured cream mixture over them and sprinkle one-half of the onion on top. Repeat the layers of potato slices, soured cream mixture and onion, then arrange the remaining potato slices on the top and pour the remaining soured cream mixture over them.

4 Cover the dish with foil and cook in a preheated oven, 180°C (350°F), Gas Mark 4, for 1 hour, then remove the foil and cook for a further 20 minutes.

5 Garnish with the paprika and the thyme sprigs, and leave to stand for about 5 minutes before serving.

serves 4

1 kg (2 lb) evenly sized floury
  potatoes, scrubbed but unpeeled

75 g (3 oz) butter

1 small mild onion, finely chopped

salt and pepper

rösti

1 Cook the potatoes in a large saucepan of lightly salted boiling water for about 7 minutes, then drain well. When the potatoes are quite cold, peel and grate coarsely into a bowl.

2 Heat 15 g (½ oz) of the butter in a large frying pan. Add the onion and cook for about 5 minutes until soft, then stir into the grated potato and season to taste with salt and pepper.

3 Melt the remaining butter in the frying pan and set aside about 1 tablespoonful of the melted butter in a cup. Add the potato mixture to the pan and form it into a neat cake. Cook gently for about 15 minutes, shaking the pan occasionally so that the rösti does not stick, until the underside is a crusty golden brown.

4 To cook the top of the rösti, pour the reserved melted butter over it and then either place the frying pan under a preheated grill to brown or turn the rösti over in the pan and brown.

5 Invert the rösti on to a warmed flat dish and cut it into wedges to serve.

colcannon

serves 4–6

1 Cook the kale or cabbage in a saucepan of lightly salted water for about 10 minutes, or until very tender. Meanwhile, cook the potatoes in another saucepan of lightly salted water until tender.

2 While the vegetables are cooking, place the spring onions or chives and the milk or cream in a saucepan and bring just to the boil, then simmer over a low heat for about 5 minutes.

3 Drain the kale or cabbage and mash. Drain the potatoes and remove the peel wearing clean rubber gloves. Mash well, then add the hot milk mixture, beating well to give a soft fluffy texture. Beat in the kale or cabbage, season with salt and pepper and add one-half of the butter. The colcannon should be a speckled green colour. Heat through thoroughly before serving in individual bowls. Make a well in the centre of each and put a knob of the remaining butter in each one. Serve immediately.

500 g (1 lb) kale, stalks removed and finely shredded, or green cabbage, cored and finely shredded

500 g (1 lb) potatoes, scrubbed but unpeeled

6 spring onions or chives, finely chopped

150 ml (¼ pint) milk or cream

125 g (4 oz) butter

salt and pepper

roast potatoes

with rosemary and garlic

serves 4

750 g (1½ lb) potatoes, scrubbed but unpeeled

4 tablespoons olive oil

2 tablespoons chopped rosemary

4 garlic cloves, peeled and sliced

salt and pepper

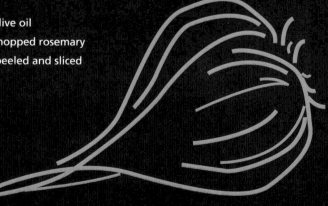

1 Cut the potatoes lengthways into quarters and pat dry with a clean tea towel.

2 Pour one-half of the oil into a large roasting tin and place on the top shelf of a preheated oven, 230°C (450°F), Gas Mark 8, for a few minutes to warm.

3 Mix together the remaining oil and the rosemary in a large bowl and toss the potatoes in the mixture to coat completely. Add the potatoes to the heated roasting tin, shaking carefully to give an even layer, then return the tin to the top shelf and roast for 20 minutes.

4 Remove the tin from the oven and move the potatoes around so that they cook evenly. Scatter the garlic slices among the potatoes, then return the tin to the oven for a further 5 minutes. Season with salt and pepper and serve immediately.

planning *ahead*

If you want to save money, don't just plough on with your same old weekly shop in the hope that this week it will miraculously be somehow cheaper. The best way to make savings is to take the time to plan before you even get to the shops. Rule number one is: always write a shopping list. Writing a list will help you to buy what you need, rather than buying too much or too little, or acting on impulse and throwing unnecessary items into the trolley because 'you might fancy it later'. So much food is wasted every week because people over-buy or plan badly and then end up throwing uneaten produce away.

What's on the list?

The best way to start a shopping list is to plan your weekly menu. When are you in, and what meals are going to be needed? Are you expecting guests, or have the kids got clubs or activities that mean that special (or extra-big) meals and snacks are going to be required?

Be realistic when you plan your menu. There's no point in thinking you'll save by not buying treats, but then craving them all week and splurging with a trip (or two) to a coffee shop for an expensive slice of cake.

Another thing to think about is unexpected guests. Be sure you've got a few storecupboard essentials (see pages 242–243) so that if you suddenly have a few more people at the dinner table, you can stretch the meal to feed everyone.

Be flexible

Once you've written your basic list, do keep an open mind as to what you buy. Flexibility is important when you're looking for bargains. The price of ingredients – particularly fresh produce – goes up and down, and quality will vary too. Often it's better to think 'fish on Tuesday' rather than deciding on a specific type of fish. The day's catch will vary, as will prices, so it's often better to make your final choice when you're there and you can see the quality and price in front of you. The same is true of fruit and veg. Think about how much you need and the type of fruit or veg (for example 'green veg to go with fish'), then make your decision on the day.

Planning for leftovers

If you want to make a gift for grandparents, it's a really nice idea to get the grandchildren involved. Try making simple cookies and get the kids to create designs on top using their (clean) fingers, or brightly coloured sweets.

•

Make double quantities of your evening meal so you can enjoy leftovers for lunch the next day.

•

Add leftover veggies to soups, stews and pasta sauces.

•

Sauté leftover potatoes for a simple accompaniment, or fry up with leftover greens to make bubble and squeak.

•

Add cold veggies, such as roast peppers or steamed green beans, to salads.

•

Toss cold rice or noodles into a stir-fry.

•

Stir leftover pasta into a veggie sauce, pop in a baking dish and sprinkle with cheese to make a hearty pasta bake.

•

Add cooked fish to pasta sauces, salads and risottos, tarts, pies or pastries, or turn them into fish cakes.

•

Use cooked meat and poultry in sandwich fillings, sauces, stews, curries, salads, omelettes, pies, risottos, pasta dishes and stir-fries, or sprinkle them over pizzas and into tarts and quiches.

Beware of impulse buys

Planning ahead and writing a list will go some way towards helping you avoid impulse buys and false 'bargains'. Supermarket shelves are packed with cut-price and multi-buy offers but you need to think about whether these bargains will actually help you save money. For example, if you eat a lot of pasta, then buying three packets for the price of two will probably be money well spent. But what about those half-price desserts you hadn't planned on buying and don't really need? Tempting they may be, but if you don't really need them – leave them on the shelf and count up the money you've already saved! And those extra-large cans of baked beans that look like such a bargain? Well it's not such a bargain if you eat only half the can and end up throwing the rest away. So, before you buy, always think:

• Do I need this?
• Will I use it?
• Can I finish it up before its use-by date?
• Have I got space to store it?

serves 4

4 tablespoons olive oil

250 g (8 oz) parsnips, cut into equal-sized chunks

250 g (8 oz) leeks, trimmed, cleaned and cut into 1 cm (½ inch) lengths

250 g (8 oz) red peppers, cored, deseeded and cut into squares

250 g (8 oz) aubergines, cut into chunks

½ teaspoon crushed dried chillies

handful of marjoram, chopped

salt and pepper

1 Pour the oil into a large roasting tin and place on the top shelf of a preheated oven, 220°C (425°F), Gas Mark 7, for a few minutes to warm.

2 Add the parsnips to the tin, tossing them well in the oil, then return the tin to the top shelf and cook for 10 minutes.

3 Remove the tin from the oven and add the leeks, red peppers, aubergines and crushed dried chillies. Toss to coat in the olive oil, then return the tin to the oven to cook for a further 15 minutes.

4 Add the marjoram and salt and pepper and mix well. Serve immediately.

roast vegetables *with* *olive oil and chillies*

honey carrots

1 Pour the water into a saucepan and add the carrots. Bring to the boil, then cover and simmer for about 10 minutes, or until the carrots are still slightly crisp. Drain. (If you are using frozen carrots, follow the packet instructions.)

2 Melt the butter in a large frying pan over a medium-high heat. Add the sugar, honey and carrots. Reduce the heat and turn the carrots frequently for 1–2 minutes until they are well glazed. Sprinkle with the parsley before serving.

serves 6

125 ml (4 fl oz) water

750 g (1½ lb) baby carrots, fresh or frozen

15 g (½ oz) butter

1 tablespoon soft light brown sugar

2 tablespoons clear honey

2–3 tablespoons finely chopped parsley

spicy stir–fried cauliflower

with almonds

serves 4

1 cauliflower

75 g (3 oz) blanched almonds

2 tablespoons vegetable oil

1 onion, finely chopped

2.5 cm (1 inch) piece of fresh root ginger, peeled and finely chopped

2 garlic cloves, crushed

2 teaspoons ground coriander

1 teaspoon turmeric

½ teaspoon chilli powder

6 tablespoons water

salt

1 Break the leaves off the cauliflower, reserving the small green frondy leaves. Separate the florets from the stalks, then break the florets into individual sprigs and slice the stalks thinly on the diagonal. Blanch the stalks and sprigs in lightly salted boiling water for 2 minutes, then drain, rinse under cold running water and drain again.

2 Heat a deep frying pan or wok until hot. Add the almonds and dry-fry over a gentle heat until toasted on all sides, then tip on to a chopping board and chop coarsely.

3 Heat the oil in the pan or wok over a moderate heat. Add the onion, ginger, garlic and spices and stir-fry for 2–3 minutes, or until softened, taking care not to let the ingredients brown.

4 Add the cauliflower sprigs and stalks, sprinkle the water over and season with salt. Increase the heat to high and stir-fry for 2–3 minutes, or until the cauliflower is tender but still crisp.

5 Taste and add more salt, if necessary. Serve at once, sprinkled with the chopped toasted almonds and garnished with the reserved green cauliflower leaves.

serves 4

250 g (8 oz) thin green beans

250 g (8 oz) mixed red and yellow baby tomatoes, plum if possible, cut in half

1 handful trimmed mint leaves, chopped

1 garlic clove, crushed

4 tablespoons extra virgin olive oil

1 tablespoon balsamic vinegar

salt and pepper

1 Cook the beans in a saucepan of lightly salted boiling water for 2 minutes, then drain well. Place in a bowl with the tomatoes.

2 Add the chopped mint, garlic, olive oil and balsamic vinegar. Season with salt and pepper and mix well. Serve warm or cold.

tomato and green bean salad

mains

serves 6

125 g (4 oz) long grain rice

1 chicken, about 1.5 kg (3 lb),
  with giblets

300 ml (½ pint) chicken stock

50 g (2 oz) raisins

1 small green pepper, cored, deseeded
  and chopped

grated rind of 1 lemon

butter, for greasing

500 g (1 lb) onions, quartered

500 g (1 lb) baby carrots

500 g (1 lb) small tomatoes, peeled
  and quartered

¼ teaspoon chopped rosemary

300 ml (½ pint) dry cider

squeeze of lemon juice

salt and pepper

boiled potatoes tossed in chopped
  parsley, to serve

stuffed
pot–roast
chicken
in cider

1 Cook the rice in lightly salted boiling water for
10 minutes, or until tender, then drain well. Remove the
chicken giblets and chop the liver, then cook for a few
minutes in a little stock. Drain. Mix together the rice,
chicken liver, raisins, green pepper, grated lemon rind
and salt and pepper. Stuff the chicken with this mixture.

2 Grease a casserole dish large enough to hold the chicken
comfortably. Place the onions, carrots and tomatoes in
the bottom and lay the chicken on top. Sprinkle the
chicken with the rosemary and pour the cider over.

3 Cover the casserole and cook in a preheated oven,
180°C (350°F), Gas Mark 4, for 2 hours until the chicken
is tender. Remove the lid for the last 10 minutes to
brown the chicken.

4 Lift the chicken out of the dish and place on a warmed
serving plate. Remove the vegetables carefully with a
slotted spoon and arrange them around the chicken.
Strain the juices from the casserole into a small pan and
add the lemon juice. Reheat and serve separately, in a
jug or sauceboat. Serve the chicken and stuffing with
boiled potatoes tossed in chopped parsley.

pork steaks
with **apples** *and*
mustard mash

serves 4

4 floury potatoes, peeled and diced

handful of sage leaves, chopped

2 tablespoons extra virgin olive oil

1 tablespoon lemon juice

1 tablespoon clear honey

1 large green apple, peeled, cored, quartered and cut into thick wedges

4 pork steaks, about 200 g (7 oz) each

50 g (2 oz) butter

2 tablespoons milk

1 tablespoon Dijon mustard

salt and pepper

1 Boil the potatoes in a saucepan of lightly salted boiling water for 10 minutes, or until tender.

2 Meanwhile, mix the sage with the oil, lemon juice and honey and season with salt and pepper. Mix one-half of the flavoured oil with the apple wedges and brush the rest over the pork.

3 Grill the steaks under a preheated medium-hot grill for 3–4 minutes on each side, until browned and cooked through. Set aside and keep warm.

4 Drain the potatoes and mash with a potato masher. Beat in 40 g (1½ oz) of the butter, the milk and mustard and season to taste with salt and pepper. Keep warm.

5 Melt the remaining butter in a frying pan and quickly fry the apple wedges for 2–3 minutes until golden and softened. Serve the pork with the mustard mash, apples and any pork juices.

buying the *best* for *less*

Getting good value for money isn't just about buying food that seems cheap, it's also about getting the most for your money. That means good quality, good flavour and the right quantity for the right price. And, of course, there's the hidden value of health as well – because there are few things more valuable than food that's good for you and good for your family.

Fabulous fruit and veg

Always go for fresh-looking ingredients with springy, lush leaves. Choose firm, healthy-looking specimens and avoid anything wilted, bruised or wrinkled or that feels too soft. Checking the ripeness of fruit varies from type to type: melons and soft fruits usually give off a sweet, fragrant scent when they're ready to eat; avocados, peaches and plums will 'give' slightly when gently squeezed; and pineapples are ready if a centre leaf comes out easily when you give it a good tug. If you're unsure, just ask your greengrocer and he'll be happy to advise.

Marvellous meat

Meat can be expensive, but if you know how to choose the right cuts, it can offer good value for money. More economical cuts such as stewing steak benefit from marinating and/or long slow cooking to get really tender results, but the bonus is that they have a great flavour, are often lean and are perfectly suited to one-pot stews and casseroles for family meals. Mince is also a good buy and can be turned into loads of dishes that all the family will love: burgers, bolognese sauce, meatballs, lasagne, shepherd's pie, moussaka...

Look out for lean cuts without much fat or gristle (because you don't want to pay for the bits you'll throw away) and buy good-quality mince. Cheaper mince is often very high in fat and will have more waste than better-quality meat.

Perfect poultry

Always buy the best-quality bird you can afford, as this usually reflects on the way the bird has been reared, and consequently its flavour. Choose plump, healthy-looking birds with blemish-free skin. Larger birds offer better value because there is a larger ration of meat to carcase.

Fantastic fish and shellfish

Always buy the freshest fish you can and, ideally, eat it on the day you buy it. Fresh fish should have glistening skin, bright eyes, firm flesh and a 'fresh' smell. If fish smells strongly, it's a good sign that it's not as fresh as it could be and you'd be better buying something else.

The importance of quality

Often it's better to spend a little more on (or buy a little less of) a good-quality ingredient than it is to buy larger quantities of a cheaper, less-flavoursome and inferior product. For example, buying a slightly more expensive cheese with a good, strong flavour may prove to be more economical than buying a big block of bland, mild cheese, since you'll need to use far more of the mild cheese to make a tangy, cheesy sauce.

Expensive ingredients such as liqueurs don't have to be off the shopping list entirely if you shop and cook wisely. If you only use a splash in cooking in a dish, the ingredient won't be that expensive. Spirits and liqueurs have a long shelf-life, so as long as it's something you'll use up gradually, consider it a storecupboard investment.

Convenience foods can be handy for families, but choose wisely. A bargain pizza or some cheap sausages may seem like a good idea, but if the kids don't think they taste nice and you end up throwing them away, or they're packed with additives, fat or sugar, where's the value in that?

Think about filling, sustaining food too. A more expensive wholegrain loaf will keep you fuller for longer than a cheap plain white loaf – and it's better for you too.

Prepare your own

It's nearly always cheaper to prepare your own fresh ingredients than it is to buy them ready prepared.

•

Cubes of fruit or vegetable sticks are easy to make yourself, so why would you pay someone else to do it for you?

•

Topping and tailing beans or slicing veg to stir-fry can be done in minutes, so why not put in a little extra time to make some big savings?

•

Buying a whole chicken and jointing it yourself is often cheaper than buying the parts of the bird separately.

•

Most fishmongers are happy to gut and clean your fish for you at no extra cost, so don't feel you have to do this job yourself.

1 Put the mustard seeds in a small, heavy-based frying pan and heat gently until they start to pop. Use a pestle and mortar to crush them lightly with the salt.

2 Cut away the skin from the squash and scoop out any seeds. Cut the squash into chunky slices.

3 Pat the pork steaks dry on kitchen paper and rub the mustard and salt mixture over the tops.

4 Melt the butter with the oil in a large, heavy-based frying pan and fry the squash for about 5 minutes on each side until golden and tender. Drain, transfer to a plate and keep warm. Add the pork steaks, spiced side down, and fry for 6–8 minutes until golden. Turn the steaks over and add the sage and stock. Cook gently for a further 6–8 minutes until cooked through. Drain the steaks and keep warm.

5 Stir the crème fraîche into the pan and cook, stirring, until it is bubbling and slightly thickened. Check the seasoning and serve with the pork and squash.

serves 4

2 teaspoons mustard seeds

¼ teaspoon sea salt

500 g (1 lb) squash, such as butternut

4 pork steaks, about 150 g (5 oz) each

25 g (1 oz) butter

1 tablespoon vegetable oil

1 tablespoon chopped sage

150 ml (¼ pint) chicken stock

100 ml (3½ fl oz) crème fraîche

pan–fried
pork with
squash

serves 4

3–4 tablespoons olive oil

25 g (1 oz) butter

500 g (1 lb) onions, sliced

1 tablespoon chopped parsley, plus extra to garnish

500 g (1 lb) calves' liver, thinly sliced

4 tablespoons beef stock

salt and pepper

chopped flat leaf parsley, to garnish

to serve

mashed potatoes

sautéed mushrooms

venetian-style
calves' liver

1 Heat the oil and butter in a frying pan, add the onions and parsley and cook gently for 2–3 minutes.

2 Add the liver, increase the heat and stir in the stock. Cook the liver for 5 minutes, then remove from the heat and season to taste.

3 Serve immediately with mashed potatoes, topped with sautéed mushrooms and garnished with parsley.

steak and *mushroom* *pie*

serves 4

3 tablespoons seasoned flour

750 g (1½ lb) stewing steak, diced

50 g (2 oz) butter

1 large onion, chopped

2 garlic cloves, crushed

450 ml (¾ pint) stout

150 ml (¼ pint) beef stock

2 bay leaves

1 tablespoon hot horseradish sauce

250 g (8 oz) closed-cup mushrooms, trimmed

milk, to glaze

salt and pepper

for the pastry

175 g (6 oz) plain flour, plus extra for dusting

pinch of salt

75 g (3 oz) chilled butter, diced

2–3 tablespoons iced water

1 Put the seasoned flour on a plate and coat the steak in it. Heat a knob of the butter in a large, heavy-based frying pan and fry the meat in batches until it is well browned, using a slotted spoon to drain and transfer each batch to an ovenproof casserole dish. Fry the onion and garlic in a little more butter until softened.

2 Add the stout, stock, bay leaves, horseradish sauce and a little salt and pepper to the frying pan. Bring to the boil and pour the mixture over the meat, then cover with a lid. Transfer to a preheated oven, 150°C (300°F), Gas Mark 2, and cook for 1½ hours until the meat is tender.

3 Meanwhile, fry the mushrooms in the remaining butter for 5 minutes and add them to the beef for the last 30 minutes. Leave the meat mixture to cool, then turn it into a 1 litre (1¾ pint) pie dish and chill, ideally overnight.

4 To make the pastry, sift the flour and salt into a large mixing bowl, add the butter and rub in with the fingertips until the mixture resembles fine breadcrumbs. Gradually add enough cold water to bind the ingredients. On a lightly floured surface, knead the dough briefly until smooth, then wrap in clingfilm and chill for 30 minutes.

5 Roll out the pastry on a lightly floured surface until it is 5 cm (2 inches) larger than the dish. Cut a long strip of pastry of the same width as the dish rim from around the edge. Wet the rim with water, using a pastry brush, and press the strip in place all around the rim. Wet the top of the pastry strip and place the remaining piece of pastry over the dish, trimming it to fit with a table knife. Press it down firmly around the edge with the tines of a fork. Brush with milk and bake in a preheated oven, 190°C (375°F), Gas Mark 5, for 45 minutes until deep golden.

1 Boil the lentils in a saucepan containing plenty of water for 15 minutes, then drain.

2 Meanwhile, heat 1 tablespoon of the oil in a frying pan and fry the onion for 5 minutes. Stir in the garlic and fry for a further 2 minutes.

3 Add the lentils, rosemary or thyme, stock and a little salt and pepper to the frying pan and bring to the boil.

4 Pour into a shallow, ovenproof dish and arrange the fish on top. Score the tops of the tomatoes and tuck them around the fish. Drizzle with the remaining oil.

5 Bake, uncovered, in a preheated oven, 180°C (350°F), Gas Mark 4, for 25 minutes, or until the fish is cooked through. Sprinkle with parsley and serve.

serves 4

150 g (5 oz) Puy lentils

3 tablespoons olive oil

1 large onion, finely chopped

3 garlic cloves, sliced

several rosemary or thyme sprigs

200 ml (7 fl oz) fish stock

4 chunky pieces of white fish fillet, skinned

8 small tomatoes

salt and pepper

2 tablespoons chopped flat leaf parsley, to garnish

braised fish with lentils

halibut
in *paper*
parcels

serves *4*

1 fennel bulb

4 halibut fillets, about 200 g (7 oz) each

2 shallots, finely chopped

8 pitted black olives

a few sage leaves, torn

4 lemon slices

salt and pepper

1 Cut 4 sheets of greaseproof paper large enough to enclose the fish and vegetables.

2 To prepare the fennel, trim the top and outer leaves, remove the hard central core and cut the bulb into slices through the root. Divide evenly between the sheets of greaseproof paper and put the fish on top. Sprinkle with the shallots, olives and sage, season with salt and pepper and finish with a slice of lemon.

3 Fold the greaseproof paper over to make a parcel, then either staple it closed or roll the edges to seal. Put the parcels on to a baking sheet and cook in a preheated oven, 200°C (400°F), Gas Mark 6, for 25 minutes.

4 Serve these parcels at the table so that everyone opens their own parcel and gets a waft of the delicious aroma that escapes when they are first opened.

using the *freezer*

The freezer is an absolute boon when you're trying to tighten your purse strings. It allows you to take advantage of seasonal produce when it's at its cheapest and most abundant best, plus it allows you the flexibility to take advantage of special offers, bulk-buying and bulk-cooking – and, of course, if you've bought something you're not going to be able to eat, you may well be able to freeze that too rather than throwing it away.

Freezing fresh ingredients

Whether you're taking advantage of well-priced seasonal treats or freezing your own home-grown produce, fresh fruit, vegetables and herbs are absolutely brilliant to freeze. Soft fruits such as berries can be frozen on a tray, then stored in freezer bags or containers. Orchard fruits such as apples can discolour when they thaw, so they are best coated in a sugar syrup (1 litre/1¾ pints water, 450g/1lb sugar and the juice of 1 lemon) before being frozen. Cooked fruits such as stewed apples and poached plums also freeze very well. Most vegetables should be blanched to preserve their colour during freezing. Prepare the vegetables as you would for cooking, then plunge into boiling water for about 2 minutes before refreshing in cold water. Pack into containers and freeze. As for herbs, these should be chopped and frozen in small freezer bags or tubs. You can then add spoonfuls of frozen herbs directly to cooked dishes.

Fish, meat and poultry are good for freezing too. Ready-frozen fish retains all the nutritional value of fresh, which makes it a good freezer choice. It also gives you flexibility as to when you want to serve it. If you want to freeze fresh fish yourself, make sure it's really fresh. Meat and poultry also freeze well and are another good standby. Be sure to thaw them slowly in the refrigerator and make sure they're thoroughly defrosted before being cooked. Interleaving individual portions such as chops and burgers with greaseproof paper means that you can remove the number you need without having to thaw the whole batch.

Freezing for another day

There are loads of ways you can take advantage of your freezer by making or buying now and eating later. Here are just a few: when making soups, stocks and stews, make several batches at a time and freeze in portion-sized quantities; take advantage of multiple-purchase offers such as 'buy one pizza, get one free' and store the extra in the freezer for another week; turn stale bread or cake into crumbs and freeze for later use.

Top tips for freezing

Always freeze in portion-sized quantities to avoid waste by thawing more than you need.

•

Always label containers with the content and date frozen.

•

Never re-freeze food that has already been thawed.

•

Freeze food quickly, ideally on the day you buy it, but thaw it slowly.

•

Use frozen foods within 3 months of freezing.

Freezer standbys

It's good to keep a well-stocked freezer for everyday meals, as well as those unexpected moments when you suddenly need extra food. Frozen vegetables, fruit and ingredients such as prawns are brilliant because they last for months so you don't need to worry about whether you need to use them up in the next few days. This flexibility is great if you suddenly change your plans for the week because you won't find yourself with an extra meal on your hands and no one to eat it. The ingredients can just wait in the freezer until next week when you're ready to cook the meal. These ingredients are also fabulous for unexpected guests because you've got extra food at the ready, even if you hadn't planned for it.

Part-baked loaves such as ciabatta and baguettes are great for unexpected guests when you need to make a meal go further, while an ordinary sliced loaf can be stored in the freezer, with slices ready to go straight in the toaster whenever you need them. Storing toasting bread in this way means you'll never end up throwing the end of the loaf away, because it's always perfectly fresh.

Keep a packet or two of pastry in the freezer for use in both sweet and savoury dishes.

Pizzas and batch dishes that you've made previously – such as soups, stews, casseroles and bakes – are great for quelling cravings for instant meals without the effort. And ice cream, sorbet and frozen yogurt are great for any occasion – but particularly when you've got guests or children screaming for a treat!

haddock
and cider casserole

serves 4

25 g (1 oz) butter

1 onion, sliced

40 g (1½ oz) plain flour

300 ml (½ pint) dry cider

2 leeks, trimmed, cleaned and sliced

375 g (12 oz) cooking apples, peeled,
    cored and sliced

750 g (1½ lb) haddock fillets, skinned
    and thickly sliced

salt and pepper

to garnish

1 apple, peeled, cored and sliced
    into rings

1 teaspoon oil, for brushing

1 tablespoon chopped parsley

1 Melt the butter in a saucepan and cook the onion over a moderate heat for 10 minutes, but do not let it brown. Stir in the flour and cook for 2 minutes.

2 Add the cider, bring to the boil and cook for 3 minutes, stirring until thickened. Season well with salt and pepper.

3 Place the leeks, apples and fish in a shallow 1.8 litre (3 pint) ovenproof dish and pour the sauce over. Cover and cook in a preheated oven, 180°C (350°F), Gas Mark 4, for 50–60 minutes.

4 Meanwhile, lightly brush the apple rings for the garnish with the oil and cook under a preheated grill until they are light golden brown on both sides. Remove from the heat and drain on kitchen paper.

5 Uncover the casserole at the end of the cooking time and garnish with the grilled apple rings and the parsley. Serve immediately.

1 Lightly beat the egg white in a shallow dish, add the strips of fish and turn to coat. Spread the cornflour out on a plate, then dip the fish in the cornflour until lightly coated on all sides.

2 In a large, heavy-based saucepan or wok, heat sufficient oil for deep-frying to 180–190°C (350–375°F), or until a cube of bread browns in 30 seconds. Deep-fry a few pieces of fish at a time for 1–2 minutes, or until golden. Lift out with a slotted spoon, drain on kitchen paper and keep hot. Repeat with the remaining strips of fish.

3 Pour off all the oil from the saucepan or wok and wipe the inside clean with kitchen paper. Add all the sauce ingredients, return to a moderate heat and bring to the boil, stirring. Simmer until the sauce has reduced slightly, then lower the heat, return the fish to the pan and heat through for 1 minute. Serve the fish and sauce on individual bowls of steamed or boiled rice.

serves 4

1 egg white

500 g (1 lb) white fish fillets, cut into chunky strips

2 tablespoons cornflour

vegetable oil, for deep-frying

steamed or boiled rice, to serve

for the sauce

125 ml (4 fl oz) fish stock

2 tablespoons soy sauce

2 tablespoons chilli sauce

1 tablespoon lemon juice

1 tablespoon tomato purée

2 teaspoons soft light brown sugar

fish fillets in *hot sauce*

serves 4

1 kg (2 lb) sweet potatoes, peeled
  and roughly cubed

1 tablespoon crushed mixed peppercorns

4 thick white fish fillets, about 150 g
  (5 oz) each

175 g (6 oz) baby spinach, torn

2 tablespoons olive oil

salt and pepper

fish with *sweet potato* and *spinach mash*

1 Steam the sweet potatoes in a steamer over boiling water for 10–15 minutes, or until just soft.

2 Meanwhile, mix some salt with the crushed peppercorns and sprinkle over one side of the fish fillets. Cook the fish, peppered side up, under a preheated hot grill for 8–10 minutes, or until they are cooked through.

3 Transfer the sweet potatoes to a bowl and mash roughly. Add the spinach, oil and salt and pepper to taste and mix together. The heat from the sweet potatoes will cause the spinach leaves to wilt into the mash.

4 Make a bed of sweet potato and spinach mash on each plate and place the fish on top.

shopping wisely

If you shop for food week-in, week-out, it's very easy to get into routines and bad habits that waste money. Are you guilty of walking down the supermarket aisles throwing in the same old produce week after week, not even checking the prices or thinking about alternatives. Well stop right there! If you're serious about managing your budget and making savings on your food bills, you need to start again – taking more interest in what you're buying and how you buy it.

Breaking bad habits

We've already talked about planning ahead and writing shopping lists (see pages 138–139), but before you get started on planning and shopping, have a look at your current shopping habits.

• What do you buy but never use? Is it that head of broccoli that you always pick up because you feel you should, but throw away at the end of the week? Is it those extra yogurts that have passed their use-by date? Or did you over-do the special offer on canned peaches – and now you've got a cupboardful that no one wants to eat?
• Do you cook the same old meals, using the same old ingredients, every week?
• Are you (or your family) scared to try new things, even though you often enjoy them when you do?
• Do you check the price of an item before putting it in your trolley?
• Do you find yourself thinking 'How on earth did I spend that much?' every time you come to pay?

Starting again

If the answer is 'yes' to any or all of the questions above, then there are plenty of ways for you to save. The easiest way is to break your bad habits and start afresh. Follow the golden rules below and you'll find you've shaved pounds off your bill. Even a few pence here and a few pence there will add up in the context of a whole week's shop.

• Buy foods you know you'll eat (and don't over-buy, or buy things that will have passed their use-by date before you get to them).
• Always check the price.
• Try different brands – often cheaper brands of the same product can be just as good.
• Be flexible – if strawberries are on special offer, why not buy those instead of the raspberries you were planning on? If courgettes are cheaper one week, why not buy those instead of the veggie accompaniment you had planned?

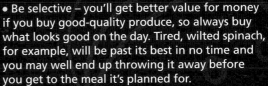

Trying new things

It can be a risk buying unfamiliar ingredients, or making unfamiliar dishes. After all, what happens if you don't like them? Well, you may well find you do like them, and the more foods and dishes you have in your everyday repertoire of meals, the more flexibility you will have with your budget. By increasing the number of ingredients you could buy and cook, you create more flexibility and options – giving you the chance to take advantage of even more bargains when they arise. And if you really don't enjoy it? Well you will have learned something and you don't have to make it again. Isn't one slightly less-enjoyable meal during the week a small price to pay for the savings you could enjoy?

• Be selective – you'll get better value for money if you buy good-quality produce, so always buy what looks good on the day. Tired, wilted spinach, for example, will be past its best in no time and you may well end up throwing it away before you get to the meal it's planned for.
• If you can't keep track of what you're spending, take a calculator with you. Tot up your shop as you go, and if you find you're overspending, make some cheaper substitutions to make sure you come in on budget when it comes to paying.

Shopping around

If you have time, it really is worth shopping around to pick up the best bargains. Supermarkets are great for staples and special offers, but you can pick up even better bargains elsewhere.

• Open-air markets and greengrocers are great for picking up good-value fruit and veg.
• Ethnic stores in the heart of ethnic communities can be great places to pick up well-priced spices, rice, pulses and exotic produce.
• Whole-food shops are often a good place to bulk-buy dry goods such as grains, pulses, dried fruit and nuts.
• Butchers and fishmongers will often offer excellent-quality produce as well as advice on cooking and preparation.

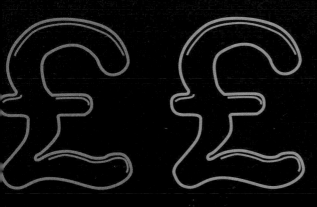

cherry tomato
tarts *with pesto*

serves 4

2 tablespoons olive oil, plus extra
for greasing

1 onion, finely chopped

375 g (12 oz) cherry tomatoes

2 garlic cloves, crushed

3 tablespoons sun-dried tomato paste

325 g (11 oz) ready-made puff pastry,
defrosted if frozen

flour, for dusting

beaten egg, for glazing

150 g (5 oz) crème fraîche

2 tablespoons ready-made pesto

salt and pepper

basil leaves, to garnish

1 Heat the oil in a frying pan, add the onion and cook for 3 minutes. Halve about 150 g (5 oz) of the tomatoes. Remove the pan from the heat and add the garlic and sun-dried tomato paste, then stir in all the tomatoes.

2 Roll out the pastry on a lightly floured surface and cut out 4 rounds, each 12 cm (5 inches) across, using a plain cutter or small bowl. Transfer to an oiled baking sheet. Use a sharp knife to mark a shallow line 1 cm (½ inch) in from the edge of each round, to form a rim. Brush the rims with beaten egg.

3 Pile the tomato mixture in the centres of the pastry cases within the rims. Bake in a preheated oven, 220°C (425°F), Gas Mark 7, for 15 minutes, or until risen and golden.

4 Meanwhile, put the crème fraîche, pesto and salt and pepper to taste in a bowl and mix lightly so that the crème fraîche is streaked with the pesto. Transfer the cooked tarts to serving plates and spoon the pesto sauce over the top. Garnish with basil leaves and serve.

1 Heat 1 tablespoon of the oil in a frying pan and fry the onion and celery for 5 minutes until softened. Put the onion and celery into a food processor, add the tofu and apricots and blend to a chunky paste.

2 Tip the mixture into a bowl and add the breadcrumbs, egg and sage. Season with salt and pepper and beat well until evenly combined. Divide the mixture into 8 portions. Using lightly floured hands, shape each portion into a sausage, pressing the mixture together firmly.

3 Heat the remaining oil in a nonstick frying pan and fry the sausages for about 5 minutes, or until golden. Serve immediately with potato wedges and tomato relish, if liked.

serves 4

2 tablespoons olive oil

1 large onion, roughly chopped

2 celery sticks, roughly chopped

225 g (7½ oz) smoked firm tofu, drained, patted dry and torn into chunks

100 g (3½ oz) ready-to-eat dried apricots, roughly chopped

50 g (2 oz) fresh white breadcrumbs

1 egg

1 tablespoon chopped sage

flour, for dusting

salt and pepper

to serve

potato wedges (optional)

tomato relish (optional)

smoked tofu and apricot sausages

chickpea
chole

serves 4—6

3 tablespoons vegetable oil

1 onion, chopped

2 garlic cloves, crushed

2.5 cm (1 inch) piece of fresh root ginger, peeled and grated

4 teaspoons ground cumin

1 tablespoon ground coriander

2 teaspoons chilli powder

1 teaspoon turmeric

2 x 410 g (13½ oz) cans chickpeas, drained and rinsed

400 g (13 oz) can chopped tomatoes

1½ teaspoons soft dark brown sugar

1–2 tablespoons lime juice (depending on taste)

4 tablespoons torn coriander leaves

salt

to garnish

3 coriander sprigs

½ red onion, sliced

1 Heat the oil in a heavy-based saucepan, add the onion, garlic and ginger and fry over a gentle heat, stirring frequently, for about 5 minutes, or until softened but not coloured.

2 Stir in the dried spices and fry for 2 minutes. Add the chickpeas, tomatoes, sugar and some salt to taste, and stir to combine. Bring to the boil, then cover and simmer gently for 10 minutes, stirring occasionally.

3 Stir in 1 tablespoon of the lime juice and the coriander leaves and heat through for a further 2 minutes. Taste the curry and add the remaining lime juice and more salt if necessary. Serve the chole hot, garnished with the coriander sprigs and red onion slices.

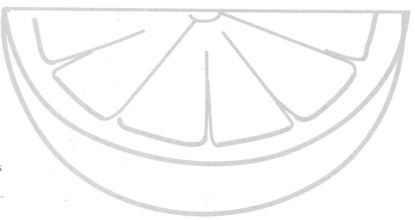

serves 4

300 g (10 oz) dried orzo

2 garlic cloves, crushed

large handful of basil leaves

5 tablespoons olive oil

rind and juice of 2 lemons

150 g (5 oz) Parmesan cheese, freshly grated

salt and pepper

1 Cook the orzo in a large saucepan of boiling water for 6–8 minutes, or according to the packet instructions.

2 Meanwhile, using a pestle and mortar, blend the garlic, basil, oil and lemon rind and juice together until smooth. Add the Parmesan, blend well and season with salt and pepper.

3 Drain the orzo thoroughly. Add the pesto and mix well so that the sauce is distributed evenly throughout the orzo. Serve immediately.

lemon and basil orzo

desserts

lavender
crème brûlées

serves 6

600 ml (1 pint) single cream

4–6 fresh lavender flower heads, depending on size

6 egg yolks

75 g (3 oz) caster sugar

2 tablespoons demerara sugar

fresh lavender sprigs, to decorate

1 Pour the cream into a small saucepan, add the lavender heads and heat gently for 2–3 minutes, but do not boil. Remove the pan from the heat and set aside for 30 minutes to infuse.

2 Put the egg yolks and caster sugar into a bowl and beat until smooth. Remove the lavender with a slotted spoon, then reheat the cream, bringing it almost up to the boil. Gradually stir the hot cream into the egg yolk mixture and then strain into a jug or back into the saucepan.

3 Pour the mixture into 6 individual ovenproof ramekins or shallow dishes, cover the tops with foil and stand them in a roasting tin. Pour in enough cold water to come halfway up the sides of the dishes and then bake in a preheated oven, 160°C (325°F), Gas Mark 3, for 25–30 minutes until just set. Take the dishes out of the roasting tin and leave to cool at room temperature, then place in the refrigerator for at least 4 hours or overnight.

4 Sprinkle 1 teaspoon of the demerara sugar over the top of each dish and cook under a preheated grill or using a cook's blowtorch for 3–5 minutes until the sugar has caramelized. Cool, then chill for 2–3 hours, but no longer, otherwise the crèmes brûlées will begin to soften and lose their wonderful crunchy texture. Decorate with lavender sprigs and serve.

serves 4

600 ml (1 pint) milk

25 g (1 oz) caster sugar

50 g (2 oz) butter

125 g (4 oz) risotto rice

50 g (2 oz) hazelnuts, toasted and chopped

50 g (2 oz) sultanas

125 g (4 oz) plain dark chocolate (at least 70% cocoa solids), grated, plus extra to decorate

splash of brandy (optional)

chocolate *risotto*

1 Put the milk and sugar in a saucepan and heat until almost boiling.

2 Meanwhile, melt the butter over a low heat in a heavy-based saucepan, add the rice and stir well to coat the grains with the butter.

3 Add the hot milk, a large ladleful at a time, stirring until each addition has been absorbed into the rice. Continue adding milk in this way over a low heat for 25–35 minutes, until all the milk has been used up and the rice is creamy but still has some bite.

4 Add the hazelnuts, sultanas, grated chocolate and a splash of brandy, if using, and mix quickly, but lightly, to give a marbled effect. Serve decorated with extra grated chocolate.

lemon and bay custards

serves 4–6

12 bay leaves, bruised

2 tablespoons grated lemon rind

150 ml (¼ pint) double cream

4 eggs plus 1 egg yolk

150 g (5 oz) caster sugar

100 ml (3½ fl oz) lemon juice

1 Put the bay leaves, lemon rind and cream in a small, heavy-based saucepan and heat gently. When it starts to boil, remove it from the heat and set aside for 2 hours to infuse.

2 Whisk together the eggs, egg yolk and sugar until the mixture is pale and creamy, then whisk in the lemon juice. Strain the cooled cream mixture through a fine sieve into the egg mixture and stir until combined.

3 Pour the custard into 4 individual ovenproof ramekins or shallow dishes and place on a baking sheet. Bake in a preheated oven, 120°C (250°F), Gas Mark ½, for 50 minutes, or until the custards are almost set in the middle. Leave until cold, then serve. If the custards are not wanted until later, chill until required, then return to room temperature before serving.

serves 4

4 oranges
175 g (6 oz) granulated sugar
125 ml (4 fl oz) water
1 small pineapple

caramelized
orange and
pineapple

1 With a very sharp knife, remove the rind from 2 of the oranges and slice it into very fine strips. Place the rind in a saucepan of boiling water and simmer for 2 minutes. Remove and drain well.

2 Put the sugar and water into a heavy-based saucepan and heat gently, swishing the pan constantly until the sugar has dissolved. Increase the heat and boil the syrup until it turns a golden brown. Take care not to overcook the caramel: if it gets too dark, carefully add 2 tablespoons of water, standing back as you do so because the caramel will spit. Set aside when ready.

3 To peel the remaining oranges, cut a slice off the top and bottom of each one, then place the orange on one of these cut sides and take a knife around the side of the orange, cutting away the skin and pith. Remove the pith from the 2 oranges from which the rind was removed in step 1 in the same way. Cut across each orange into about 6–7 slices.

4 To prepare the pineapple, top and tail it and slice away the skin from top to bottom. Make sure that you remove the 'eyes' close to the skin. Cut the pineapple into quarters and remove the core. Cut into slices.

5 Make alternate layers of orange and pineapple in a heatproof dish. Sprinkle with the orange rind and pour over the caramel, then leave to stand until required.

serves 6

450 ml (¾ pint) unsweetened
  red grape juice

2 x 12 g (½ oz) sachets
  powdered gelatine

50 g (2 oz) caster sugar

500 g (1 lb) bag frozen mixed
  berry fruits

1 Pour 150 ml (¼ pint) of the grape juice into a heatproof
  bowl and sprinkle the gelatine over the top, making sure
  it has all been absorbed. Leave to stand for 10 minutes.

2 Set the bowl over a saucepan of simmering water and
  stir until the gelatine has completely dissolved. Stir the
  sugar into the gelatine mixture, then mix with the
  remaining grape juice.

3 Pour the still-frozen fruits into a 1 kg (2 lb) loaf tin,
  cover with the warm juice mixture and mix together.
  Chill in the refrigerator for 3 hours until the jelly has
  set and the fruits have defrosted completely.

4 To serve, dip the loaf tin into a bowl of just-boiled
  water. Count to 10, then run a knife around the edge
  of the jelly and turn it out on to a serving plate. Serve
  the jelly cut into thick slices.

red berry
terrine

pears
with
chocolate
crumble

serves 4

50 g (2 oz) light muscovado sugar

150 ml (¼ pint) water

25 g (1 oz) raisins

½ teaspoon ground cinnamon

4 ripe dessert pears, peeled, halved and cored

40 g (1½ oz) unsalted butter

50 g (2 oz) porridge oats

25 g (1 oz) hazelnuts, roughly chopped

50 g (2 oz) milk or plain dark chocolate, chopped

lightly whipped cream or Greek yogurt, to serve (optional)

1 Put one-half of the sugar in a large frying pan with the water, raisins and cinnamon. Bring just to the boil and add the pears, then simmer gently for 5 minutes, or until the pears are slightly softened.

2 Meanwhile, melt the butter in a separate frying pan or saucepan. Add the porridge oats and cook gently for 2 minutes. Stir in the remaining sugar and cook over a low heat until golden.

3 Spoon the pears on to serving plates. Stir the hazelnuts and chocolate into the oat mixture. Once the chocolate starts to melt, spoon the mixture over the pears. Serve topped with whipped cream or Greek yogurt, if you like.

dine in

Eating out — at home

It's Saturday, and you'd really like to go out to dinner tonight, or at least have a take-away, but the budget won't allow it. Rather than go without, just decide which kind of food you'd like to eat – Italian, Mexican, Indian, Thai or Chinese – and then prepare a fantastic meal right there in your own kitchen. The family will love it, and so will your purse and your waistline, as homemade is nearly always less fattening. We've chosen dishes from some of the most popular cuisines that are easy to make, and not too expensive, so you'll have money to spare for a nice bottle of wine. And don't let the fact that you're staying in make it less of an occasion: get your glad rags on, set the table with style and enjoy!

italian

margherita
pizzas

serves 4

for the dough

150 ml (¼ pint) warm water

1 teaspoon dried active yeast

250 g (8 oz) strong white bread flour, plus extra for dusting

pinch of caster sugar

1 teaspoon sea salt

1 tablespoon extra virgin olive oil, plus extra for greasing

for the topping

500 g (1 lb) ripe plum tomatoes, skinned, deseeded and diced

2 tablespoons chopped basil

2 garlic cloves, crushed

½ teaspoon dried oregano

pinch of dried chilli flakes

1 tablespoon olive oil

300 g (10 oz) mozzarella cheese, grated

25 g (1 oz) Parmesan cheese, freshly grated

6 canned anchovy fillets in oil, drained and chopped (optional)

salt and pepper

1 Put the warm water in a bowl, add the yeast and stir until it dissolves. Stir in 4 tablespoons of the flour and the sugar and leave in a warm place for 10 minutes until really frothy.

2 Sift the remaining flour into a mixing bowl, add the salt and make a well in the centre. Gradually work in the yeast mixture and oil to form a soft dough, then knead for 8–10 minutes on a lightly floured surface.

3 Shape the dough into a ball and place in an oiled bowl. Cover with oiled clingfilm and leave to rise in a warm place for 1 hour, until doubled in size.

4 Meanwhile, to make the topping, place the tomatoes, basil, garlic, oregano, chilli flakes and olive oil in a bowl and stir well. Cover and leave to marinate for 30 minutes.

5 Tip the dough on to a lightly floured surface and punch it a few times to knock the air out of it, then knead lightly to shape into a ball. Divide it into 4 equal pieces and roll one piece out thinly to form a 23 cm (9 inch) round. Transfer to a well-floured board or baking sheet and top each pizza with one-quarter of the tomato mixture, mozzarella, Parmesan and anchovies, if using, then season with salt and pepper.

6 Carefully slide the pizza straight on to a preheated baking sheet or pizza stone in a preheated oven, 240°C (475°F), Gas Mark 9, and bake for about 10–12 minutes, until the base is cooked and the topping is bubbling.

7 Prepare the second pizza while the first one is cooking, and so on with all 4. Serve the pizzas as soon as they are cooked.

1 Put one pizza base at a time on a well-floured board or baking sheet and brush with a little of the oil. Arrange one-quarter of the vegetables on the base and sprinkle with one-quarter of the thyme and basil. Season the pizza well with salt and pepper and drizzle with one-quarter of the remaining oil.

2 Carefully slide the pizza straight on to a preheated baking sheet or pizza stone in a preheated oven, 230°C (450°F), Gas Mark 8, and bake for 10 minutes until the base is cooked and the topping is bubbling. The vegetables should be slightly charred around the edges, as this adds to the flavour.

3 Prepare the second pizza while the first one is cooking, and so on with all 4. Serve the pizzas as soon as they are cooked, with Parmesan shavings, if you like.

fresh vegetable pizzas

serves 4

4 x 23 cm (9 inch) pizza bases (see Margharita Pizzas on page 184)

5 tablespoons olive oil

2 garlic cloves, crushed

1 red onion, thinly sliced

2 courgettes, thinly sliced lengthways

1 red pepper, cored, deseeded and cut into thin strips

1 yellow pepper, cored, deseeded and cut into thin strips

4 plum tomatoes, skinned, cored and cut into small wedges

500 g (1 lb) fine asparagus tips

4 thyme sprigs, leaves stripped

handful of basil leaves, roughly torn

salt and pepper

75 g (3 oz) Parmesan cheese, freshly shaved (optional), to serve

tomato bruschetta

serves 2

1 Lightly toast the ciabatta slices on both sides under a preheated high grill, then brush with a little oil.

2 Arrange the mozzarella and tomatoes on the toast and scatter the basil over the top.

3 Cook the bruschetta under the grill until the cheese has melted slightly. Serve immediately.

6 thick slices of ciabatta

olive oil, for brushing

125 g (4 oz) mozzarella cheese, thinly sliced

24 cherry tomatoes, diced

a few basil leaves, torn into small pieces

spinach *and* ricotta *gnocchi*

with chilli–butter dressing

serves 4

750 g (1½ lb) spinach, thick stalks removed

175–250 g (6–8 oz) ricotta cheese

2 egg yolks

175 g (6 oz) Parmesan cheese, freshly grated

¼ teaspoon freshly grated nutmeg

2 sage leaves, plus 6–8, chopped, to garnish

50 g (2 oz) plain flour, plus extra for dusting

salt and pepper

125 g (4 oz) Parmesan cheese, freshly grated, to garnish

for the dressing

75 g (3 oz) butter

1 small red chilli, deseeded and finely chopped

1 Place the spinach in a pan with just the water that clings to the rinsed leaves. Cover and cook for a few minutes until the leaves are wilted and tender. Increase the heat to drive off any remaining water. Tip into a colander, squeeze dry with a wooden spoon and leave to cool.

2 To make the gnocchi mixture, put the spinach, ricotta, egg yolks, Parmesan, nutmeg, sage leaves and salt and pepper in a food processor or liquidizer and blend until smooth. Turn into a bowl, sift the flour over the mixture and mix to form a dough. Cover with clingfilm and place in the refrigerator for about 15 minutes.

3 Meanwhile, to make the chilli-butter dressing, melt the butter and gently fry the chilli in it until soft. Keep warm.

4 Using well-floured hands, take 15 g (½ oz) pieces of the gnocchi mixture and shape them into 24 small ovals or egg shapes. As each gnocchi is made, place it on a lightly floured tray until ready to cook.

5 Fill a large, wide pan with lightly salted water and bring to the boil, then reduce the heat to a simmer. Poach 6 gnocchi at a time for 4–5 minutes until they are puffed and have risen to the surface. Remove with a slotted spoon and pile into warmed individual dishes.

6 Drizzle the chilli butter over the gnocchi, sprinkle with the Parmesan and chopped sage leaves and serve immediately.

fancy foods *for less*

Just because you're cooking on a budget, there's no reason to think you can't rustle up meals fit for a king (or queen). Whether you're making a family meal, creating a romantic dinner for two or throwing a dinner party, there are loads of ways to dress up even the simplest and cheapest of ingredients.

From frugal to fabulous

Turn an ordinary meal into dinner-party fare by putting in a little planning time, thought and ingenuity. What could have been an unadventurous mid-week supper might be ideal for entertaining. The easiest way is to plan three courses, or put a little extra effort into the accompaniments.

Making a simple pasta supper? How about serving the salad accompaniment as a starter instead of piling it on the plate alongside the pasta, and ring the changes by trying a new or exotic dressing?

Find ways of livening up veg. Instead of serving boring old boiled potatoes as an accompaniment, why not get creative? Try sautéing them in olive oil and garlic instead, or slicing thinly and layering with chopped garlic and a drizzle of cream before baking. Or what about roast potatoes? As for green veg – steam them and then top with a good knob of butter and sprinkle with fresh herbs.

Really impress your guests by cooking a themed meal (see pages 180–251). For example, start with spring rolls, serve a stir-fry or Thai curry for the main course, then finish with a tropical fruit salad. Indian, Italian, Mexican, Chinese, Thai ... whatever you choose, your guests will love it!

Simple starters

Rustling up quick, easy, affordable starters is the simplest way to make a meal seem more special. Start off with one of the following:

slices of toasted baguette topped with chopped tomatoes, garlic, fresh basil and olive oil to make Italian-style bruschetta

•

a bowl of fresh leafy salad

•

a ready-made dip served in a bowl and accompanied by crisps or vegetable sticks

•

a small tartlet or wedge of quiche with a salad garnish

•

a wedge of fresh melon

•

pâté served with wafer-thin slices of toast

•

grilled field mushrooms drizzled with olive oil and sprinkled with chopped garlic and black pepper

•

a small bowl of soup

Stunning desserts

You can make show-stopping desserts with very little effort or money. Just tweak some old favourites:

•

Fill a Victoria sandwich with whipped cream and fresh berries and dust with icing sugar.

•

Dress up a fruit salad with slices of more expensive tropical fruit or a handful of fresh berries, and, for an adult meal, add a splash of dessert wine or liqueur.

•

Top scoops of ice cream or other creamy desserts with dark chocolate curls.

•

Serve simple desserts such as ice cream and fruit salads with delicate biscuits or cookies.

•

Make individual trifles with stale cake and leftover fruit salad.

Creating luxurious meals for less

Adding a small quantity of a more expensive ingredient can often work wonders in transforming a relatively ordinary dish into something special. For example, a single bunch of asparagus spears, cut into lengths, will elevate the luxury level of loads of simple, inexpensive dishes such as pasta or risotto. Similarly, a small packet of tiger prawns goes a long way in a Thai vegetable curry or fresh, leafy salad and will add a hint of luxury to an otherwise simple meal. In the same vein, top risottos and pasta dishes with shavings of Parmesan or crumbled blue cheese, or stir smoked salmon trimmings into scrambled eggs, use to fill quiches and tarts or add to a creamy pasta sauce for an intense flavour and pretty colour with less cost. Finally, note that olives will add an air of sophistication to pasta sauces, salads and other dishes, and need not be expensive.

Perfect presentation

Turning a simple meal into something sensational is often just about the presentation. Starting with the table: dress it with candles and flowers (if your budget will extend that far), and use a tablecloth if you have one. Dress the food, too, to make your meal less everyday and more spectacular, by adding a simple garnish such as fresh herbs, crispy croutons, breadcrumbs or snipped crispy bacon, a drizzle of dressing or fruit coulis, a sprinkling of citrus zest, or a dusting of icing sugar or cocoa powder. Also, arrange side salads in individual bowls, rather than creating a big salad bowl for everyone to dig into. Finally, transform an everyday pudding such as apple crumble or trifle into a special dessert just by preparing and serving it in individual dishes.

lasagne
al forno

serves 4

9 sheets ready-to-cook lasagne

50 g (2 oz) Parmesan cheese, freshly grated

for the meat sauce

2 tablespoons vegetable oil

2 onions, finely chopped

3 garlic cloves, crushed

1 tablespoon dried oregano

1 tablespoon dried basil

3 tablespoons tomato purée

500 g (1 lb) minced beef

400 g (13 oz) can chopped tomatoes

salt and pepper

for the cheese sauce

25 g (1 oz) butter

25 g (1 oz) plain flour

600 ml (1 pint) milk

250 g (8 oz) Cheddar cheese, grated

salt and pepper

to serve

green salad

crusty bread

1 To make the meat sauce, heat the oil in a large saucepan and fry the onions for 3–5 minutes until soft. Add the garlic and fry for 1 more minute, then stir in the herbs, tomato purée and beef. Fry, stirring constantly, for 5 minutes. Add the tomatoes and a dash of salt and pepper and stir well, then cover the pan and simmer for 45 minutes, stirring occasionally.

2 Meanwhile, make the cheese sauce. Melt the butter in a heavy-based saucepan, stir in the flour and cook over a low heat for 1 minute. Remove the pan from the heat and gradually add the milk, stirring constantly. Once all the liquid has been incorporated, return the pan to a low heat and bring to the boil, stirring constantly until the sauce is smooth and thick. Leave to simmer for a few minutes, then add the Cheddar and a pinch of salt and pepper.

3 Grease a 1.8 litre (3 pint) ovenproof dish. Spoon one-third of the meat mixture over the base, then spread one-quarter of the cheese sauce on top and cover with 3 sheets of lasagne. Do the same twice more, finishing with a layer of lasagne. Cover with the rest of the cheese sauce and sprinkle the Parmesan over the top. Bake in a preheated oven, 190°C (375°F), Gas Mark 5, for 1 hour until browned and bubbling. Serve with a green salad and crusty bread to mop up the juices.

1. Put the lamb, onion, oregano, breadcrumbs and a little salt and pepper in a bowl and mix together well by hand. Shape the mixture into small balls about 3 cm (1¼ inches) in diameter.

2. Heat the oil in a large frying pan and gently fry the meatballs, shaking the pan frequently, for 8–10 minutes, or until they are browned.

3. Remove the meatballs with a slotted spoon and set aside. Add the garlic, tomatoes, sugar, chilli powder, lemon rind and salt and pepper to the pan. Heat gently, stirring, until the mixture is bubbling.

4. Return the meatballs to the pan, cover with a lid and cook gently for 10 minutes, or until the meatballs are cooked through and tender. Serve immediately with freshly cooked pasta.

serves 4

500 g (1 lb) lean minced lamb

1 large red onion, finely chopped

2 tablespoons finely chopped oregano

50 g (2 oz) fresh white breadcrumbs

3 tablespoons olive oil

3 garlic cloves, crushed

500 g (1 lb) tomatoes, skinned and chopped, or 400 g (13 oz) can chopped tomatoes

1 teaspoon caster sugar

1 teaspoon mild chilli powder

finely grated rind of 1 lemon

salt and pepper

freshly cooked pasta, to serve

meatballs
in a *spicy* sauce

spaghetti *carbonara*

serves 4

2 eggs, plus 4 egg yolks

150 ml (¼ pint) single cream

50 g (2 oz) Parmesan cheese, freshly grated

2 tablespoons olive oil

100 g (3½ oz) pancetta or streaky bacon, finely sliced

2 garlic cloves, crushed

400 g (13 oz) fresh spaghetti

salt and pepper

1 Beat together the eggs and yolks, cream, Parmesan and plenty of pepper.

2 Heat the oil in a large frying pan and fry the pancetta or bacon for 3–4 minutes, or until golden and turning crisp. Add the garlic and cook for a further 1 minute.

3 Meanwhile, cook the spaghetti in a large saucepan of lightly salted boiling water for 2 minutes, or until tender.

4 Drain the spaghetti and tip it straight into the frying pan. Turn off the heat and stir in the egg mixture until the eggs are lightly cooked. (If the heat of the pasta doesn't quite cook the egg sauce, turn on the heat and cook briefly, stirring, but do not overcook or it will resemble scrambled eggs.) Serve immediately.

butternut squash risotto

serves 4

125 g (4 oz) butter

3 tablespoons olive oil

1 garlic clove, finely chopped

1 onion, finely diced

300 g (10 oz) risotto rice

1 litre (1¾ pints) hot chicken or vegetable stock

1 butternut squash, weighing about 1 kg (2 lb)

150 g (5 oz) Parmesan cheese, freshly grated

a little pumpkin seed oil

salt and pepper

1 Melt 50 g (2 oz) of the butter with 1 tablespoon of the oil in a heavy-based saucepan. Add the garlic and onion and sauté gently for 5 minutes until softened but not coloured. Add the rice and stir well to coat the grains with oil and butter.

2 Add the hot stock, a large ladleful at a time, stirring until each addition has been absorbed into the rice. Continue adding stock in this way over a low heat for about 20 minutes until the stock has all been absorbed and the rice is creamy but still has bite.

3 Meanwhile, cut the top and bottom off the squash and cut it around the middle, then pare away the skin from the larger half without losing too much of the flesh. Cut in half lengthways, remove the seeds and cut the flesh into 1.5 cm (¾ inch) dice. Repeat with the other piece. Place on a large baking sheet, drizzle with the remaining olive oil and season with salt and pepper. Mix well and cook in a preheated oven, 220°C (425°F), Gas Mark 7, for 15 minutes until soft and slightly browned.

4 When the risotto is ready, add the squash, Parmesan and remaining butter, season to taste with salt and pepper and stir gently. Cover the pan and leave the risotto to rest for a few minutes before drizzling a little pumpkin seed oil on top of each portion and serving.

serves 4

4 tablespoons strong espresso coffee

2 tablespoons grappa or brandy

10 sponge fingers

175 g (6 oz) mascarpone cheese

2 eggs, separated

50 g (2 oz) icing sugar, sifted

25 g (1 oz) plain dark chocolate, finely grated

mint leaves, to decorate

1 Combine the coffee and grappa or brandy in a shallow bowl and dip the sponge fingers into the liquid to coat them evenly. Arrange the fingers in a small, shallow dish, pouring any excess liquid over them.

2 In a bowl, whisk together the mascarpone, egg yolks and icing sugar until smooth and well blended. In another bowl, whisk the egg whites until stiff and glossy, then fold into the mascarpone mixture until well blended.

3 Spoon the mixture over the sponge fingers and smooth the surface. Sprinkle the chocolate on top. Cover and chill until set. Decorate with mint leaves.

tiramisu

mexican

spicy nachos *with* cheese

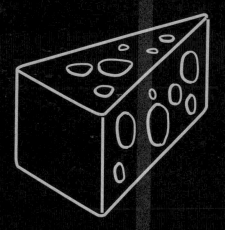

serves 4–6

250 g (8 oz) tortilla chips

125 g (4 oz) Cheddar cheese, grated

for the chilli sauce

2 tablespoons olive oil

1 onion, chopped

2 garlic cloves, crushed

4 large tomatoes, skinned, deseeded and chopped

2 jalapeño chillies, deseeded and chopped

pinch of dried oregano

pinch of ground cumin

salt and pepper

to garnish

2 spring onions, cut into strips

1 red chilli, deseeded and cut into strips

1 To make the chilli sauce, heat the oil in a small saucepan and sauté the onion and garlic until soft and golden, stirring occasionally. Add the remaining sauce ingredients and bring to the boil, then simmer gently for 15 minutes, or until the chilli sauce is thickened and reduced.

2 Arrange the tortilla chips on a large ovenproof dish or plate and carefully spoon the chilli sauce over the top of them. Sprinkle with the Cheddar and cook in a preheated oven, 180°C (350°F), Gas Mark 4, for 10–15 minutes, or until the cheese melts and starts to bubble.

3 Meanwhile, soak the spring onion and chilli strips in very cold water for 5–10 minutes to make them curl. Serve the nachos garnished with spring onion and chilli curls.

grow *your own fruit and veg*

If you really want to cut down on your fresh produce bill, the best way is to grow your own – whether that's fruit, veg or herbs, or all three! Growing your own also means you can choose whether to go organic or to use chemical fertilizers. Don't worry if you think you don't have enough space available, because there really isn't any space too small (or dark) that you can't put to good use. How about:

• a pot of herbs on the windowsill
• a window box full of herbs, or a tub on the terrace
• grow bags on a patio or deck for tomatoes and courgettes
• a plastic dustbin for early potatoes
• a veggie patch in your garden where you can grow anything from potatoes and root veg to lettuces, peas and strawberries
• fruit trees such as apples and plums …
• … and if you don't have a single light, sunny space, you can always nurture a box of mushrooms in the cellar.

Planning and planting

The cheapest way to grow your own is to buy packets of seeds, which are very affordable. However, if you're new to gardening or doubtful of your skill and green fingers, you might want to begin with seedlings that a garden centre has already started off for you. You will get many kilos of produce from the seeds or seedlings, so the savings available are clear.

When you decide to embark on growing your own fruit and veg, you should sit down and do a little planning first. Decide which produce you want to grow, then find out when they need to be planted and harvested. Once you have this information, you're ready to plan and plant your vegetable patch.

A word of warning, though: although it's tempting to get on and plant all your seeds and seedlings at the same time, remember that if you plant everything at the same time, in all likelihood, you'll be harvesting them at the same time too. And do you really want ten tomato plants full of ripe tomatoes ready at the same time? To avoid this, try planting in phases and choosing produce that will be ready at different times, so you have a regular source of fresh, perfectly ripe produce just when you need it.

Coping with seasonal gluts If you do find you've over-planted and you suddenly have far too much produce and not enough mouths to feed, don't despair: there are plenty of ways to make good use of your seasonal glut.

• Fresh fruit, veg and herbs are great for freezing – whether you freeze them as they are or turn them into dishes first (see pages 158 and 212).
• Cook a batch of preserves – there's bound to be a jam, chutney, relish or pickle that's just perfect for your extra produce.
• Swap produce with other people who grow their own. You're bound to have too much of different crops, and while you'll be delighted with some courgettes, they'll welcome your surfeit of peppers with open arms.

Great food to grow

The best thing about growing your own is the excitement of watching your plants blossom, bloom and ripen. Some plants are easier to grow than others, but good choices, particularly for fledgling gardeners, are:

- robust herbs, such as chives, sage and rosemary
- tubers and root vegetables, such as potatoes, carrots, beetroot and turnips
- winter vegetables, such as cabbage and broccoli
- onions and leeks
- summer vegetables, such as tomatoes, courgettes, marrows, peas, beans and sweetcorn
- soft fruits, such as strawberries and raspberries.

Pick your own

If growing your own sounds like just too much effort, you can still save money by picking someone else's. Plenty of local farmers and producers offer 'pick your own' schemes where you can go and pick as much as you want – and because you do the work, it ends up cheaper.

Don't forget wild foods too. Go blackberry picking in late summer/autumn and turn the results into desserts or preserves, and pick sloe berries in late autumn to turn into ruby-red sloe gin. When gathering wild foods, do be careful that you know exactly what you're picking and that it's edible. (This is particularly important if you gather wild mushrooms, as many are toxic.)

Allotments

If you're a keen gardener and have plenty of time on your hands, but only have a small garden, think about getting an allotment, where you will be able to plant and grow a much larger range and quantity of produce. Most areas have allotment schemes, and although demand for them is high, it's well worth getting your name down on the waiting list because a plot will become free sooner or later.

serves 4

2 tablespoons olive oil

2 large onions, thinly sliced

2 garlic cloves, crushed

2 red peppers, cored, deseeded and thinly sliced

2 green peppers, cored, deseeded and thinly sliced

4 green chillies, deseeded and thinly sliced

2 teaspoons chopped oregano

250 g (8 oz) button mushrooms, trimmed and sliced

salt and pepper

to serve

12 warmed tortillas

salsa and soured cream

vegetable
fajitas

1   Heat the oil in a large frying pan and gently sauté the onions and garlic for 5 minutes until soft and golden brown. They should be melting and almost caramelized.

2   Add the peppers, chillies and oregano and stir well. Sauté gently for 10 more minutes until cooked and tender.

3   Add the mushrooms and cook quickly for 1 more minute, stirring to mix thoroughly with the other vegetables. Season with salt and pepper to taste.

4   To serve, spoon the sizzling hot vegetable mixture into the warmed tortillas and fold over or roll up. Serve very hot with salsa and plenty of soured cream.

tostadas

serves 4

1 Put the minced beef in a frying pan and fry it gently in its own fat until it is cooked and browned, breaking it up as it cooks. Pour off and discard any excess fat.

2 Add the chillies, garlic, cumin, tomato purée, stock and vinegar to the pan and bring to the boil, stirring. Add the tomatoes, reduce the heat and cook gently for 10–15 minutes until reduced and thickened.

3 Meanwhile, heat about 5mm (¼ inch) oil in a large frying pan and fry the tortillas for about 1 minute on each side until they are crisp and golden.

4 Place a large spoonful of the meat mixture on each fried tortilla (tostada), top with the lettuce, cheese and olives and serve.

500 g (1 lb) minced beef

2 red chillies, deseeded and chopped

2 garlic cloves, crushed

½ teaspoon ground cumin

125 ml (4 fl oz) tomato purée

175 ml (6 fl oz) beef stock

1 tablespoon vinegar

2 tomatoes, skinned and chopped

olive oil, for shallow-frying

8 tortillas

shredded lettuce

grated cheese

stoned black olives

serves 4—6

2 tablespoons olive oil

3 onions, chopped

1 red pepper, cored, deseeded and diced

1 green pepper, cored, deseeded and diced

2 garlic cloves, crushed

500 g (1 lb) lean minced beef

450 ml (¾ pint) beef stock

¼–1 teaspoon chilli powder

2 x 410 g (13½ oz) cans kidney beans, drained and rinsed

400 g (13 oz) can chopped tomatoes

½ teaspoon ground cumin

salt and pepper

flat leaf parsley, to garnish

to serve

soft tortillas

soured cream

pickled green chillies

Cheddar cheese, grated (optional)

chilli con carne

1 Heat the oil in a heavy-based saucepan or flameproof casserole. Add the onions, peppers and garlic and fry gently until soft. Add the beef and fry until just coloured. Stir in the stock and add the chilli powder, beans, tomatoes and cumin. Season with salt and pepper.

2 Bring the mixture to the boil, then cover and simmer very gently for 50–60 minutes, stirring occasionally.

3 Serve the chilli con carne wrapped in soft tortillas, garnished with parsley and accompanied by the soured cream, green chillies and Cheddar, if liked.

churros

serves 4–6

150 g (5 oz) butter, diced

300 ml (½ pint) water

150 g (5 oz) plain flour

3 eggs, plus 1 egg yolk

grated rind of 1 orange

sunflower oil, for deep-frying

1 tablespoon ground cinnamon

150 g (5 oz) caster sugar

1 Put the butter into a large saucepan with the water. Heat the water gently until the butter melts and then bring to a rolling boil.

2 Sift the flour at least twice and, as soon as the water boils, tip it into the pan. Remove the pan from the heat and beat the flour into the butter and water. Continue beating until the mixture forms a ball and leaves the sides of the pan clean. Leave to cool a little and then beat in the eggs, the extra yolk and the orange rind.

3 In a large, heavy-based saucepan or wok, heat sufficient oil for deep-frying to 180–190°C (350–375°F), or until a cube of bread browns in 30 seconds.

4 Spoon the mixture into a piping bag fitted with a large star nozzle and pipe 15 cm (6 inch) lengths into the hot oil, 3–4 at a time. Fry for 2 minutes on each side, until golden brown, then remove from the oil with a slotted spoon and drain on kitchen paper.

5 Mix the cinnamon and sugar together and sprinkle over the warm churros.

indian

potato *and* fenugreek samosas

serves 6

175 g (6 oz) plain flour, plus extra for dusting

pinch of salt

75 g (3 oz) chilled butter, diced

about 4 tablespoons iced water

ghee or vegetable oil, for deep-frying

mango chutney, to serve

for the filling

6 tablespoons ghee or vegetable oil

1 large onion, finely chopped

1 green chilli, deseeded and finely chopped

2 teaspoons turmeric

2 teaspoons ground cumin

2 teaspoons ground coriander

2.5 cm (1 inch) piece of fresh root ginger, peeled and grated

2 tablespoons dried fenugreek

375 g (12 oz) potatoes, peeled and finely diced

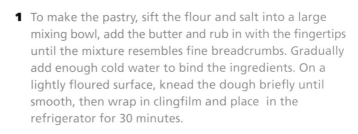

1 To make the pastry, sift the flour and salt into a large mixing bowl, add the butter and rub in with the fingertips until the mixture resembles fine breadcrumbs. Gradually add enough cold water to bind the ingredients. On a lightly floured surface, knead the dough briefly until smooth, then wrap in clingfilm and place in the refrigerator for 30 minutes.

2 Meanwhile, heat the ghee or oil in a large frying pan, add the onion and cook until soft and beginning to brown. Add the chilli, turmeric, cumin, coriander and ginger and stir-fry for 2–3 minutes. Add the fenugreek and potatoes and cook for a further 8–10 minutes, stirring frequently. Remove from the heat and leave to cool.

3 Knead the samosa pastry once more and divide into 12 walnut-sized balls. Keeping the remaining balls covered with a tea towel, flatten one ball on a lightly floured surface and roll out to a 15 cm (6 inch) circle. Cut the circle in half and form each semi-circle into a cone shape, sealing the edge with water. Fill the cavity with 2 teaspoons of the potato mixture and turn the top side over, again sealing with water. Repeat with the remaining pastry and filling.

4 In a large, heavy-based saucepan or wok, heat sufficient ghee or oil for deep-frying to 180–190°C (350–375°F), or until a cube of bread browns in 30 seconds. Slide 2 samosas into the oil and cook for 2 minutes on one side, then turn and cook until the second side is golden brown. Remove with a slotted spoon, drain on kitchen paper and keep warm while you deep-fry the remaining samosas in the same way. Serve warm with mango chutney.

eating seasonally

Choosing to eat in season is one of the best ways to get great-value fresh produce. When fruit and vegetables are in season, they should be in plentiful supply and therefore cheaper than when produce is scarce or flown in from distant climes. Not only should they be better value, but they should taste better too. Fresh produce that is allowed to mature naturally and is eaten soon after it's picked will have a much better flavour than ingredients that have been reared at speed, or stored in a warehouse for days or even weeks.

Keeping it local

Buying in season means that you can buy locally grown produce. When ingredients are out of season, supermarkets and other suppliers have to stock fruit and veg from further afield – adding extra costs of transport to your bill. But it's not just kind to your pocket – cutting back on transport and fuel is kinder to the environment too.

One of the easiest ways to shop seasonally and locally is getting involved in a local box delivery scheme. Many local producers will deliver a box of fresh, locally grown seasonal produce to your door, usually with recipe suggestions on how to cook it.

Ringing the changes

Many people worry that eating in season will mean munching on the same old meals for months on end. But eating seasonally can actually inject a variety into your weekly menus that was sadly lacking before. When you look at what's available in a certain month, you might find yourself trying new ingredients you don't usually cook with and making recipes that you haven't cooked before.

Even ordinary, everyday ingredients can be transformed into a wonderful array of different and varied dishes. Think of the humble leek: you can transform it into a wealth of fabulous dishes and meals by adding it to soups and stews, using it in frittatas or quiches or turning it into creamy tarts, pies and pastries. Or what about plums? In late summer and early autumn when they're at their juicy, flavoursome best, use them in tarts, pies, crumbles and charlottes, or turn them into sorbets and ice creams. Eat them fresh, or try them hot – baked, poached or stewed. You'll never get tired of any ingredients when there are so many different ways to cook and eat them.

Taking advantage of seasonal plenty

When fruit and veg are in season, they can cost a fraction of the price of their out-of-season cousins. So why not stock up for later months?

- Transform fruit and veg into preserves.
- Turn vegetables into soups, sauces and other dishes to freeze and enjoy in the coming months.
- Poach fruit and freeze for later.
- Check out more tips and ideas for freezing fresh produce on pages 158–159.

What's in season?

Use this handy table to check out what's in season when. (Don't forget, though, that plenty of fruit and veg such as apples, pears, carrots, onions, potatoes and beetroot are available from cold store at other times of year so still offer good value.)

	spring	summer	autumn	winter
fruit				
apples			●	
blackberries			●	
blackcurrants		●		
blueberries		●		
cherries		●		
cranberries			●	●
figs			●	
gooseberries		●		
grapes			●	
medlars			●	
melons		●	●	
peaches		●	●	
pears			●	
plums			●	
pomegranates			●	
quinces			●	
raspberries		●		
redcurrants	●	●		
rhubarb				●
strawberries		●		
white currants		●		
vegetables				
Asian greens	●		●	●
asparagus	●			
aubergines		●	●	
beans		●	●	
beetroot		●	●	
broccoli		●	●	
Brussels sprouts			●	●
cabbage	●	●	●	●
carrots	●	●	●	
cauliflower	●	●	●	●
celeriac			●	●

	spring	summer	autumn	winter
celery			●	
chicory	●		●	●
corn		●	●	
courgettes		●	●	
cucumber		●	●	
fennel			●	
globe artichokes	●	●	●	
Jerusalem artichokes				●
kale				●
kholrabi		●	●	●
leeks	●		●	●
morels	●			
okra		●		
onions			●	
parsnips			●	●
peas		●		
peppers		●		
potatoes	●		●	●
pumpkins			●	
purple-sprouting broccoli	●			
salsify			●	●
shallots		●	●	
spinach	●	●	●	●
spring onions	●	●	●	●
summer squash		●	●	
swede			●	●
sweet potatoes			●	●
Swiss chard	●	●	●	●
tomatoes		●	●	
turnips			●	●
watercress	●	●	●	●
wild mushrooms			●	
winter squash			●	●

lamb *and* courgette koftas

serves 4

2 courgettes, finely grated

2 tablespoons sesame seeds

250 g (8 oz) minced lamb

2 spring onions, finely chopped

1 garlic clove, crushed

1 tablespoon chopped mint

½ teaspoon ground mixed spice

2 tablespoons dried breadcrumbs

1 egg, lightly beaten

ghee or vegetable oil, for shallow-frying

salt and pepper

lemon wedges, to garnish

1 Place the courgettes in a sieve and press down to extract as much liquid as possible, then tip into a bowl.

2 Dry-fry the sesame seeds in a large frying pan for 1–2 minutes, or until they are golden and release their aroma. Add them and all the remaining ingredients to the courgettes, seasoning liberally with salt and pepper.

3 Form the mixture into 20 small balls. Heat about 5 mm (¼ inch) ghee or oil in a large frying pan and fry the koftas in batches for 5 minutes, turning frequently until they are evenly browned. Keep the first batch of koftas warm in a hot oven while you cook the rest. Serve garnished with lemon wedges.

tandoori *chicken*

serves 4

4 large chicken quarters, skinned
lime or lemon wedges, to garnish

for the marinade
200 ml (7 fl oz) natural yogurt
1 teaspoon grated fresh root ginger
2 garlic cloves, crushed
1 teaspoon garam masala
2 teaspoons ground coriander
¼ teaspoon turmeric
1 tablespoon tandoori masala
4 tablespoons lemon juice
1 tablespoon vegetable oil
sea salt

1 Put the chicken in a non-metallic, shallow, ovenproof dish and make 3 deep slashes in each piece, to allow the flavours to penetrate. Set aside.

2 In a bowl, mix together the marinade ingredients and spread the mixture all over the chicken pieces. Cover and leave to marinate in the refrigerator for a few hours, but ideally overnight.

3 Bake the chicken in a preheated oven, 240°C (475°F), Gas Mark 9, for 20 minutes or until cooked through. Serve garnished with lime or lemon wedges.

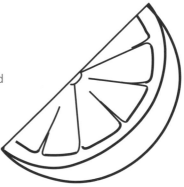

spinach dhal

serves 4

1 Place the lentils in a large saucepan with the water, turmeric and ginger and bring to the boil. Skim off any scum that forms on the surface, then lower the heat and cook gently for 20 minutes, stirring occasionally. Add the spinach and coriander leaves, stir and cook for another 8–10 minutes.

2 Heat the ghee or oil in a small, nonstick frying pan and, when it is hot, add the garlic, dried spices and chilli. Stir-fry over a high heat for 2–3 minutes, then tip this mixture into the lentils, stir to mix well and season. Serve immediately with rice or naan bread.

250 g (8 oz) red lentils, rinsed and drained

1.2 litres (2 pints) water

¼ teaspoon turmeric

1 teaspoon finely grated fresh root ginger

100 g (3½ oz) baby spinach leaves, chopped

large handful of coriander leaves, chopped

2 teaspoons ghee or light olive oil

5 garlic cloves, finely sliced

2 teaspoons cumin seeds

2 teaspoons mustard seeds

1 tablespoon ground cumin

1 teaspoon ground coriander

1 red chilli, deseeded and finely chopped

sea salt

boiled rice or naan bread, to serve

1 Melt the ghee or butter in a large frying pan. Add the onions, peppercorns, cardamoms and cinnamon and fry for about 8–10 minutes, stirring occasionally, until the onions are golden.

2 Add the ginger, garlic, chilli powder, paprika and salt to taste and fry for 2 minutes, stirring occasionally.

3 Add the chicken pieces and fry until they are evenly browned, then gradually add the yogurt, stirring constantly. Cover and cook for about 30 minutes, or until the chicken is cooked through. Serve garnished with parsley and lime wedges.

kashmiri
chicken

serves 4–6

50 g (2 oz) ghee or butter

3 large onions, thinly sliced

10 peppercorns

10 cardamom pods

5 cm (2 inch) piece of cinnamon stick

5 cm (2 inch) piece of fresh root ginger, peeled and chopped

2 garlic cloves, finely chopped

1 teaspoon chilli powder

2 teaspoons paprika

1.5 kg (3 lb) skinless chicken pieces

250 ml (8 fl oz) natural yogurt

salt

to garnish

chopped parsley

lime wedges

spicy beef in yogurt

serves 4

500 g (1 lb) braising or stewing steak
1 teaspoon salt
300 ml (½ pint) natural yogurt
175 g (6 oz) ghee or butter
1 large onion, sliced
3 garlic cloves, sliced
1½ teaspoons ground ginger
2 teaspoons ground coriander
2 teaspoons chilli powder
½ teaspoon ground cumin
1½ teaspoons turmeric
1 teaspoon garam masala
boiled rice, to serve

1 Place the beef between 2 sheets of greaseproof paper and beat until thin with a rolling pin or mallet.

2 Rub the beef with the salt, then cut into serving-sized pieces. Place in a bowl and cover with the yogurt. Cover and leave to marinate overnight in the refrigerator.

3 Melt the ghee or butter in a heavy-based saucepan and add the onion and garlic. Fry gently for 4–5 minutes until soft. Add the spices and fry for a further 3 minutes, stirring constantly.

4 Add the beef and the marinade to the pan and stir well. Bring to the boil, then cover tightly and simmer for 1½ hours, or until the meat is tender. Serve with rice.

vegetable
biriyani

serves 4—6

3 tablespoons ghee or vegetable oil

50 g (2 oz) paneer, cut into cubes

1 large onion, finely chopped

2 garlic cloves, chopped

8 cloves

5 cm (2 inch) piece of cinnamon stick

4 green cardamom pods

1 teaspoon turmeric

1 teaspoon garam masala

500 g (1 lb) basmati rice, pre-soaked
for 20 minutes

250 g (8 oz) mixed diced vegetables,
e.g. carrots, cauliflower, okra,
courgettes and green beans

600 ml (1 pint) vegetable stock

125 g (4 oz) chopped mixed nuts,
e.g. almonds, cashews, pistachios

50 g (2 oz) sultanas

salt

1 Heat the ghee or oil in a large saucepan and fry the paneer until golden, then set aside on kitchen paper. Next, fry the onion until golden, then remove one-half and set aside for the garnish. Add the garlic and spices to the pan and fry for 2–3 minutes.

2 Rinse the rice in several changes of water and drain well. Add to the pan, stir well and cook for 5 minutes until all the grains are glistening and translucent.

3 Add the mixed diced vegetables, salt and stock. Bring to the boil, then cover and reduce the heat to a bare simmer. Cook gently for 20–25 minutes until all the liquid has been absorbed and the rice is cooked.

4 Add the paneer, nuts and sultanas, and mix well. Cover and cook for 5 minutes over a low heat until all the moisture has gone. Serve hot, sprinkled with the reserved fried onion.

serves 4

150 g (5 oz) dried milk powder

50 g (2 oz) self-raising flour

2 teaspoons baking powder

5–6 tablespoons cold water

16 pistachio nuts, shelled, plus extra, chopped, to serve

oil, for deep-frying

edible gold leaf, to decorate

for the sugar syrup

500 g (1 lb) caster sugar

600 ml (1 pint) water

juice of ¼ lemon

3 cardamoms, bruised

1 tablespoon rosewater

1 To make the sugar syrup, put the sugar and water into a saucepan and heat until the sugar dissolves, then add the lemon juice and cardamoms. Bring to the boil and cook to a thick syrup. Remove from the heat and pour one-half of the syrup into a bowl to cool. Return the remaining syrup to the heat and simmer very gently.

2 Sift the milk powder, flour and baking powder into a bowl. Add the water, a teaspoon at a time, until it forms a soft dough, then knead lightly on a floured surface for 5 minutes. Cover the dough with clingfilm and leave for 30 minutes, then divide it into 16 balls and stuff each ball with a pistachio. Meanwhile, add the rosewater to the cooled sugar syrup and place in the refrigerator.

3 In a large, heavy-based saucepan or wok, heat sufficient oil for deep-frying until a cube of bread turns golden brown in 4 minutes. Add 4 dumplings to the oil and fry slowly, turning occasionally, until they are evenly reddish brown in colour, then remove with a slotted spoon and place in the simmering sugar syrup for 5 minutes. Finally, place the dumplings in the chilled sugar syrup.

4 Repeat the frying, simmering and chilling process with the remaining dumplings, then place the bowl of syrup-soaked dumplings in the refrigerator and leave for at least 1 hour. Serve sprinkled with pistachio nuts and decorated with gold leaf.

rosewater
dumplings

thai

chicken
satay

serves 4

3 tablespoons vegetable oil

1 small onion, finely chopped

2.5 cm (1 inch) piece of fresh root ginger, peeled and finely chopped

1 garlic clove, crushed

500 g (1 lb) boneless, skinless chicken thighs, cut into bite-sized pieces

1 teaspoon chilli powder, or to taste

2 tablespoons crunchy peanut butter

2 tablespoons chilli sauce

½ block creamed coconut, coarsely chopped

300 ml (½ pint) hot water

1 teaspoon soft dark brown sugar

¼ teaspoon salt

1 Heat a wok until hot. Add the oil and heat over a medium heat until hot. Add the onion, ginger and garlic and stir-fry for about 2–3 minutes, or until softened, taking care not to let the ingredients brown.

2 Add the chicken, increase the heat to high, and stir-fry for 3–4 minutes, or until lightly coloured on all sides. Sprinkle in the chilli powder, add the peanut butter and chilli sauce and stir to mix.

3 Add the creamed coconut a few pieces at a time and stir-fry until melted. Gradually add the hot water and bring to the boil, stirring all the time. Add the sugar and salt, then continue stir-frying for 5 minutes, or until the sauce is thickened. Serve hot.

thai *fish cakes* *serves 4*

500 g (1 lb) fish fillets (such as salmon, cod or haddock), cooked and flaked, bones removed

1 garlic clove, crushed

2.5 cm (1 inch) piece of fresh root ginger, peeled and finely diced

2 red chillies, deseeded and chopped

bunch of coriander, chopped

2 teaspoons Thai fish sauce (nam pla)

1 egg yolk

250 g (8 oz) mashed potato

flour, for dusting (optional)

oil, for shallow-frying

1 Place the fish, garlic, ginger, chillies, coriander, fish sauce and egg yolk in a food processor or liquidizer and blend until smooth. Remove to a bowl, add the mashed potato and mix together thoroughly with a fork.

2 Shape the mixture into 12 medium-sized fish cakes (or 24 smaller ones), dusting your hands with flour if the mixture is sticky.

3 Heat the oil in a frying pan, add the fish cakes and fry for 2–3 minutes on each side or until golden brown and heated through.

1. Heat a wok until hot. Add the oil and heat over a low heat until hot. Add the ginger and shallots and stir-fry for about 3 minutes, or until softened. Add the green curry paste and fry for a further 2 minutes.

2. Add the chicken to the wok and stir to coat evenly in the spice mixture, then fry for 3 minutes to seal the chicken. Stir in the coconut milk and bring the mixture to the boil, then reduce the heat and cook gently, stirring occasionally, for 10 minutes or until the chicken is cooked through and the sauce has thickened.

3. Stir in the fish sauce, sugar, lime leaves and chilli and cook the curry for a further 5 minutes. Taste and adjust the seasoning, if necessary, and serve the curry immediately, garnished with Thai basil leaves, if liked.

serves 4

2 tablespoons groundnut oil

2.5 cm (1 inch) piece of fresh root ginger, peeled and finely chopped

2 shallots, chopped

4 tablespoons ready-made Thai green curry paste

625 g (1¼ lb) skinless, boneless chicken thighs, cut into 5 cm (2 inch) pieces

300 ml (½ pint) canned coconut milk

4 teaspoons Thai fish sauce (nam pla)

1 teaspoon palm sugar or light muscovado sugar

3 kaffir lime leaves, shredded

1 green chilli, deseeded and sliced

Thai basil leaves, to garnish (optional)

thai green chicken curry

pad *thai*

1 Heat a wok until hot. Add 2 tablespoons of the oil and heat over a medium heat until hot. Add the tofu and stir-fry until golden brown on all sides, then add the garlic, noodles, carrot, vinegar, soy sauce and water, stirring continuously.

2 Push the contents of the wok to one side, leaving a space into which to break the eggs. Pierce the yolks and stir the eggs around, gradually incorporating the noodle mixture.

3 Pour the remaining oil into the wok and add the rest of the ingredients. Cook for 2–3 minutes, stirring and shaking the wok all the time.

4 To serve, heap the noodle mixture on to a plate and sprinkle with the peanuts. Serve with the bean sprouts and spring onion halves.

serves 4

3 tablespoons groundnut oil

175 g (6 oz) ready-fried tofu, diced

1 tablespoon chopped garlic

125 g (4 oz) bean thread noodles, soaked and drained

25 g (1 oz) carrot, grated

2 tablespoons distilled white vinegar or Chinese rice vinegar

2 tablespoons soy sauce

100 ml (3½ fl oz) water

2 eggs

1 tablespoon caster sugar

2 spring onions, sliced

¼ teaspoon ground black pepper

to garnish

1 tablespoon crushed roasted peanuts

125 g (4 oz) bean sprouts

1 spring onion, sliced in half lengthways

getting the quantities right

Often we waste food – and money – just because we cook too much and end up throwing the rest away. (Alternatively, we find we're piling on the pounds because our portions are too big and we feel we should eat all the food we've cooked.) There's no perfect solution, because appetites can vary from day to day depending on how busy and active we've been. This is particularly true when you're cooking for a family – as different people's appetites vary, and kids can be ravenous one day and only want to pick the next.

How much should we be eating?

Take the quantities below as an average for an adult, and then reduce or increase according to hunger levels. If you're cooking for a number of people, take the time to ask 'How hungry are you today?' It'll only take a moment, but it will help you to prepare the right amount of food and reduce the amount you waste. Of course, if all else fails, check out some of the many ideas for using up leftovers in this book.

Carbs Healthy-eating guidelines say about one-third of the food we eat should be made up of healthy carbohydrates, going for wholegrain varieties where possible. For an average portion of carbs allow:
- 50 g (2 oz) dried rice
- 50–75 g (2–3 oz) dried pasta
- 225 g (7½ oz) potatoes
- 2 slices wholegrain bread

Fruit and veg Aim to eat at least five portions of these a day. One portion equals: 80 g (2¾ oz) fruit or vegetables (though excluding potatoes and other tubers); 150 ml (5 fl oz) fruit or vegetable juice; 1 heaped tablespoon dried fruit; 1 dessert bowl of salad. For optimum goodness, choose fruit and veg of different colours, such as some orange carrots, red strawberries, white leeks, green peppers, yellow bananas and purple grapes.

Protein foods Our daily protein needs vary with our age: children aged 4–6 need 15–20 g (½–¾ oz); children aged 7–10 need 23–28 g (about 1 oz); women need 36–45 g (about 1½ oz); and men need 44–55 g (about 2 oz). Protein foods contain different amounts of protein, so use these guides to check you're getting the right amount:
- 1 portion (about the size of a pack of playing cards) of chicken breast, lean meat or white fish, or a small can of tuna, contains 24–27 g (about 1 oz) protein
- 1 egg contains 6 g (¼ oz) protein
- 1 regular cheese sandwich contains about 17 g (½ oz) protein
- 150 ml (¼ pint) milk contains 5 g (¼ oz) protein
- 3 tablespoons cooked pulses, such as lentils, contain 9 g (about ⅜ oz) protein
- 100 g (3½ oz) tofu contains 23 g (1 oz) protein

Try using these quantities as a guideline and see if they're right for you and your family. The first few times you use this method, cook extra carbs just to make sure you've made enough food. If there's not quite enough, increase the portions slightly; if there's too much, reduce them slightly.

Looking for patterns

Appetites, particularly in children, can sometimes seem like a mystery. Often they're driven by growth spurts or similar processes in the body, but often they're also guided by what your kids have been up to during the day. A trip to the swimming baths or a game of football can bring on a definite attack of the munchies, and when they come out of school they're bound to be starving, so try to have a healthy snack all ready for them. If there seems to be a pattern, try to use that to guide the quantities you cook and see if you end up making the right amount to eat. It isn't an exact science, so you'll still get it wrong sometimes — but looking out for patterns is certainly worthwhile.

Managing the unexpected

Even with the best-laid plans, you can often find you need to adjust your quantities at the last minute. Unexpected guest – or three? Check out the ideas below for 'stretching' your quantities and making them go that little bit further.

• Not enough meat or fish to go round? Instead of roasting, grilling or baking as you had originally planned, cut it into pieces and make it into a stew or soup, adding extra potatoes and vegetables.

• Add more veggies or beans to a curry and serve with naan bread as well as rice.

• Make a roast dinner go further by surrounding the chicken with sausages wrapped in bacon and roasting extra potatoes and veggies.

• Turn a small pan of bolognese into a large pan of chilli con carne by adding more tomatoes, kidney beans and a good pinch of chilli powder.

• Serve desserts such as tarts, pies, crumbles and fruit salads with a scoop of ice cream to make a small serving seem larger.

• Not enough wine for a party? Don't panic: combine white wine with fruit juice and a splash of brandy or vodka to make a cocktail.

1 Using a pestle and mortar, pound the chillies and garlic together until well broken down.

2 Heat a wok until hot. Add the oil and heat over a medium heat until hot. Add the chillies and garlic and stir-fry over a medium heat for 30 seconds. Add all the remaining ingredients and stir-fry for 4 minutes, then increase the heat to high and stir-fry for a further 30 seconds.

3 Turn the stir-fry on to a serving dish and serve with boiled rice, garnished with the chilli shreds.

minced chicken
with chilli and basil

serves 4

5 small green chillies, plus 1 extra chilli cut into fine shreds to garnish

2 garlic cloves

2 tablespoons vegetable oil

125 g (4 oz) minced chicken

1 shallot, chopped

25 g (1 oz) bamboo shoots

25 g (1 oz) red pepper, cored, deseeded and chopped

15 g (½ oz) carrot, diced

1 teaspoon palm sugar or light muscovado sugar

3 tablespoons Thai fish sauce (nam pla)

3 tablespoons chicken stock

15 g (½ oz) basil leaves, finely chopped

boiled rice, to serve

serves 4

25 g (1 oz) sticky (glutinous) rice

300 g (10 oz) minced beef

5 thin slices of fresh root ginger

3 tablespoons finely chopped
    spring onion

1 teaspoon chilli powder

3–4 tablespoons lemon juice

3 tablespoons Thai fish sauce (nam pla)

½ teaspoon palm sugar or light
    muscovado sugar

4–5 mint sprigs, leaves chopped,
    plus extra sprigs to garnish

3 tablespoons chopped shallots

1 crisp lettuce, separated into
    leaves, to serve

beef and ginger salad

1 Dry-fry the rice in a frying pan over a low to medium heat, shaking and stirring constantly until golden brown. Remove from the heat and leave to cool. Grind the rice in a clean spice or coffee grinder or using a mortar and pestle. Set aside.

2 Put the minced beef in a wok or saucepan and cook over a low heat for 10–15 minutes, stirring constantly, until the meat is broken up and cooked and all the liquid has been absorbed. Transfer the beef to a bowl and stir in all the remaining ingredients, except the lettuce, mixing well.

3 Arrange a bed of lettuce on a shallow dish and top with the beef mixture. Garnish with mint sprigs and serve immediately.

fried *rice* *with* *beans* and *tofu*

serves 4

groundnut oil, for deep-frying

125 g (4 oz) ready-fried tofu, diced

2 eggs

250 g (8 oz) cold boiled rice

1 tablespoon palm sugar or light muscovado sugar

1½ tablespoons soy sauce

2 teaspoons crushed dried chillies

1 teaspoon Thai fish sauce (nam pla)

125 g (4 oz) fine green beans, finely chopped

coriander leaves, to garnish

1 In a large, heavy-based saucepan or wok, heat sufficient oil for deep-frying to 180–190°C (350–375°F), or until a cube of bread browns in 30 seconds. Deep-fry the tofu until golden brown on all sides, then remove it with a slotted spoon, drain on kitchen paper and set aside.

2 Pour off all but 2 tablespoons of the oil from the pan. Heat the remaining oil until hot, then crack the eggs into it, breaking the yolks and stirring them around.

3 Add the rice, sugar, soy sauce, crushed dried chillies and fish sauce and increase the heat to high. Stir-fry vigorously for 1 minute.

4 Reduce the heat and add the green beans and tofu. Increase the heat again and stir-fry vigorously for 1 minute. Turn out on to a serving dish and garnish with coriander.

serves 4

groundnut oil, for deep-frying

750 g (1½ lb) bananas

1–2 tablespoons caster sugar

vanilla ice cream or caramel sauce, to serve

for the batter

200 ml (7 fl oz) water

150 g (5 oz) rice flour or plain flour

125 g (4 oz) grated fresh coconut or desiccated coconut

½ teaspoon salt

75 g (3 oz) palm sugar or light muscovado sugar

1 egg

banana fritters

1 Put all the batter ingredients in a bowl and beat them together.

2 In a large, heavy-based saucepan or wok, heat sufficient oil for deep-frying to 180–190°C (350–375°F), or until a cube of bread browns in 30 seconds. Meanwhile, peel the bananas, cut each one lengthways into thirds, then cut each third crossways to make slices about 7 cm (3 inches) long.

3 Coat the banana slices with the batter and slide them carefully into the hot oil, 3 or 4 at a time. Deep-fry for 3–4 minutes until golden brown. Remove with a slotted spoon and drain on kitchen paper.

4 When all the banana slices are cooked, arrange them on a serving dish and sprinkle with caster sugar. Serve immediately with vanilla ice cream or caramel sauce.

chinese

serves 4–6

250 g (8 oz) plain flour, plus
   1 tablespoon mixed to a paste
   with 1 tablespoon water

pinch of salt

1 egg

about 300 ml (½ pint) cold water

sunflower oil, for shallow- and
   deep-frying, and for greaing

for the filling

1 tablespoon sunflower oil

250 g (8 oz) lean pork, shredded

1 garlic clove, crushed

2 celery sticks, sliced

125 g (4 oz) mushrooms, trimmed
   and sliced

2 spring onions, chopped

125 g (4 oz) bean sprouts

125 g (4 oz) cooked peeled prawns

2 tablespoons light soy sauce

spring
rolls

1 Sift the flour and salt into a bowl and beat in the egg and the water until you have a smooth batter. Lightly oil a 20 cm (8 inch) frying pan and set it over a medium heat.

2 Pour in sufficient batter to cover the base of the pan. Cook until the underside is pale golden and then turn the pancake over and cook the other side. Repeat until all the batter is used, stacking the cooked pancakes between sheets of greaseproof paper to keep them warm.

3 To make the filling, heat a wok until hot. Add the oil and heat over a medium heat until hot. Add the pork and stir-fry for 2–3 minutes until it is evenly browned, then add the garlic and vegetables and stir-fry for 2 minutes. Mix in the prawns and soy sauce, then remove the pan from the heat and leave to cool.

4 Place 2–3 tablespoons of the filling in the centre of each pancake. Fold in the sides and roll up tightly, sealing the edge with a little of the flour and water paste. In a large, heavy-based saucepan or wok, heat sufficient oil for deep-frying to 180–190°C (350–375°F), or until a cube of bread browns in 30 seconds. Deep-fry the spring rolls in the hot oil, 2 at a time, until evenly golden. Drain on kitchen paper and serve hot.

1 Break the eggs into a small bowl and add 1 teaspoon of the spring onions and a pinch of the salt. Beat together lightly with a fork to combine.

2 Heat a wok until hot. Add about 1 tablespoon of the oil and heat over a medium heat until hot. Add the beaten egg mixture and stir constantly until the eggs are scrambled and set. Tip into a bowl and set aside.

3 Heat the remaining oil in the wok and add the prawns, meat, bamboo shoots, peas and the remaining spring onions. Stir-fry briskly for 1 minute, then stir in the soy sauce and stir-fry for another 2–3 minutes.

4 Add the cooked rice with the scrambled eggs and the remaining salt. Stir well to break up the scrambled eggs into small pieces and to separate the grains of rice. Serve when the rice is heated through.

special
egg-fried *rice*

serves 4

2–3 eggs

2 spring onions, finely chopped, plus extra to garnish

2 teaspoons salt

3 tablespoons vegetable oil

125 g (4 oz) cooked peeled prawns

125 g (4 oz) cooked chicken or pork, diced

50 g (2 oz) bamboo shoots, roughly chopped

4 tablespoons cooked peas

1 tablespoon light soy sauce

375–500 g (12 oz–1 lb) cold cooked rice

chow *mein*

1 Cook the noodles according to the packet instructions. Drain and rinse under cold running water until cool. Set aside.

2 Heat a wok until hot. Add about 3 tablespoons of the oil and heat over a medium heat until hot. Add the onion, meat, mangetouts or beans and the bean sprouts and stir-fry for about 1 minute. Add salt to taste and stir a few more times, then transfer the mixture to a bowl with a slotted spoon and keep hot.

3 Heat the remaining oil in the wok and add the spring onions and the noodles, together with about one-half of the meat and vegetable mixture. Stir in the soy sauce, then stir-fry for 1–2 minutes, or until heated through.

4 Divide the chow mein between 4 warm bowls, then arrange the remaining meat and vegetable mixture on top. Sprinkle with sesame oil or chilli sauce (or both, if preferred) and serve immediately.

serves 4

500 g (1 lb) dried egg noodles

4 tablespoons vegetable oil

1 onion, thinly sliced

125 g (4 oz) cooked pork, chicken or ham, cut into thin shreds

125 g (4 oz) mangetouts or French beans, trimmed

125 g (4 oz) bean sprouts

2–3 spring onions, finely shredded

2 tablespoons light soy sauce

1 tablespoon sesame oil or chilli sauce

salt

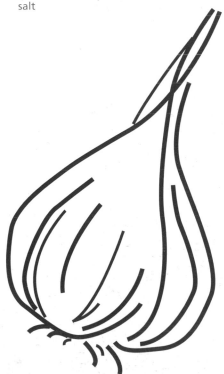

storecupboard basics

Using your storecupboard efficiently is a great way to make the most of a limited budget. A lot depends on how much storage space you have – but even with a limited space you can still make your storecupboard work for you.

Identifying the basics
• Dried accompaniments such as rice, couscous, pasta and noodles are great for any number of meals and you'll find you use them constantly through the week. Try different varieties such as white and brown rice, egg and rice noodles and long and short pasta.
• Canned fruits and vegetables can be added to either sweet desserts or savoury main meals and are incredibly versatile.
• Dried or canned beans are healthy, wholesome and incredibly versatile – suiting pasta sauces, stews, curries, soups and salads. They're also great for blending into creamy dips.
• Dried fruit and nuts are good for snacking on, but make fabulous ingredients too. Try adding dried fruit to meat stews, or throwing nuts into curries and stir-fries.
• Olive oil is great for cooking, drizzling and making dressings, while less strongly flavoured oils such as sunflower are good for cooking – particularly Asian-style dishes.
• Flour, even if you don't bake cakes or make pastry, is essential for many dishes – whether it's thickening a soup or stew or making a cheese sauce.
• Sugar is an essential for desserts, baking and preserving, and is also needed for some savoury dishes – as well as for adding to tea and coffee.

• Spices, herbs and other flavourings are an important element of the storecupboard – helping to add flavour and interest to your cooking – whether it's chilli and cumin, dried oregano, a splash of soy sauce or a spoonful of pesto.

Bulk buys
If you have plenty of space to store dried and canned goods with a long shelf-life, this is a great way to take advantage of bargain bulk items. Usually, it's cheaper – gram for gram – to buy a larger container than a smaller one. You can also take advantage of multiple-buy offers.

When buying dried goods with a shorter shelf life, such as spices and nuts, unless you use them very frequently, it may be more economical to buy smaller quantities, more regularly. There's no saving made if you buy an economy pack but don't manage to use it up before it's past its best.

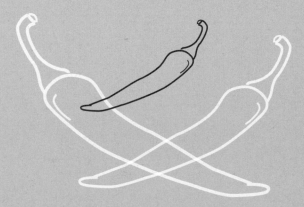

Using your storecupboard

Storecupboard ingredients are fantastic for making everyday meals, but they're even better in an emergency! Whether it's because all your careful planning has gone to waste and you suddenly find you're a meal short, or unexpected guests drop round – you won't need to panic if you have a well-stocked storecupboard, because you'll still be able to find a meal in there, or stretch the one you have.

Most meals rely on the storecupboard to some extent, whether it's for an accompaniment of pasta, rice or noodles, a can of tomatoes or a carton of coconut cream. However, you can make whole meals using only storecupboard ingredients too. What about tuna, anchovies and sun-dried tomatoes tossed in with rice, or maybe a simple bowl of spaghetti and pesto sauce? Or a hearty and wholesome bean stew made with canned tomatoes, dried herbs and pre-chopped garlic?

However, the time when your storecupboard really comes in handy is when you find yourself with unexpected guests. You can stretch the simplest meals to feed more people with just a few extras from the storecupboard.

• Add an extra can of tomatoes or beans to sauces, stews and soups to make them go further, then cook extra quantities of your chosen accompaniment – be it pasta, rice or couscous.

• Make a chicken stir-fry or pilaff go further by throwing in a handful of cashew nuts and more rice or noodles, plus extra flavourings such as Thai curry paste, sweet chilli sauce or soy sauce.

• If you're increasing your quantities of risotto rice, try adding extra veg. Chicken or prawn risottos are fabulous with the addition of canned asparagus, frozen peas or sweetcorn, while a can of tomatoes also gives wonderful results.

Easy storecupboard meals

There are hundreds of different meals you can make from storecupboard ingredients, but here are just a few quick and tasty ones that use the most basic ingredients:

•

spaghetti with tomato sauce

•

tomato and chickpea curry with rice

•

tuna pasta bake

•

lentil stew with couscous

•

sardines on toast

•

risotto (with dried mushrooms or canned asparagus)

•

sweetcorn chowder

chinese
five–spice
spare ribs

serves 4

groundnut or vegetable oil, for deep-frying

750 g (1½ lb) spare ribs, chopped into 7.5 cm (3 in) pieces

600 ml (1 pint) chicken stock

½ teaspoon Chinese five-spice powder

½ tablespoon caster sugar

4 tablespoons hoisin or plum sauce

2 teaspoons yellow bean sauce

4 tablespoons Chinese rice wine

3 garlic cloves, crushed

2.5 cm (1 inch) piece of fresh root ginger, peeled and finely chopped

2 shallots, finely chopped

2 tablespoons dark soy sauce

1 tablespoon cornflour

1 In a large, heavy-based saucepan or wok, heat sufficient oil for deep-frying until a cube of bread browns in 3 minutes. Add the spare rib pieces and deep-fry for 6–8 minutes, or until golden brown and crisp. Remove with a slotted spoon and drain on kitchen paper.

2 Put all the remaining ingredients except for the soy sauce and cornflour in a large saucepan and heat gently to dissolve the sugar. Mix the cornflour with a little water and stir it into the sauce. Bring the sauce to the boil and boil until thickened, then add the spare ribs and simmer gently, uncovered, for 45 minutes, or until tender.

3 Put a wire rack on a baking sheet. Remove the ribs from the sauce and place on the rack, then brush with plenty of the sauce. Roast in a preheated oven, 200°C (400°F), Gas Mark 6, for 15 minutes, or until piping hot and browning slightly.

fried *eight-piece* chicken

serves 4

1 chicken, about 1.25 kg (2½ lb)

2–3 spring onions, finely chopped

2–3 slices of fresh root ginger, finely chopped

2 tablespoons dry sherry

1 tablespoon sugar

3 tablespoons soy sauce

3 tablespoons cornflour

125 g (4 oz) lard

1 teaspoon sesame oil

chopped chives, to garnish

1 Wash the chicken inside and out and pat dry with kitchen paper. Carefully cut off the legs, wings and breasts, then cut each breast in half.

2 In a large bowl, mix together the spring onions and ginger with 1 tablespoon of the sherry, 1 teaspoon of the sugar and 1 tablespoon of the soy sauce. Add the chicken pieces and turn in the marinade until well coated. Leave to marinate for about 5 minutes.

3 Spread the cornflour out on a plate, remove the chicken from the marinade (reserving any leftover marinade) and coat each piece in the cornflour.

4 Meanwhile, heat a wok until hot. Add the lard and heat over a medium heat until hot, then add the chicken and fry until golden brown all over and cooked through.

5 Pour off the excess lard, add the remaining sherry, sugar and soy sauce and the leftover marinade and bring to the boil, stirring. Stir in the sesame oil, then garnish the chicken pieces with chives and serve immediately.

1 Mix together the soy sauce, sherry, sugar and flour in a large bowl. Add the spare rib pieces and set aside in a cool place to marinate for 10–15 minutes.

2 Heat a wok until hot. Add the oil and heat over a medium heat until hot. Add the spare ribs and stir-fry for a few minutes until they are golden brown. Remove with a slotted spoon and drain on kitchen paper.

3 Add the garlic, spring onions and bean sauce to the wok and stir well. Add the spare ribs with the water and cook, covered, over a high heat for 5 minutes. Add a little more liquid, if necessary, replace the lid and cook for a further 5 minutes.

4 Add the peppers and stir well. Cook for 2 minutes, then remove from the heat and serve immediately.

pork in *black bean* sauce

serves 4

1 tablespoon soy sauce

2 tablespoons dry sherry

1 tablespoon caster sugar

1 tablespoon plain flour

500 g (1 lb) spare ribs, chopped into small pieces

3 tablespoons oil

1 garlic clove, crushed

2 spring onions, sliced diagonally

2 tablespoons crushed black or yellow bean sauce

5 tablespoons water

1 small green pepper, cored, deseeded and sliced

1 small red pepper, cored, deseeded and sliced

egg-fried noodles with vegetables and tofu

serves 4

vegetable oil, for deep-frying

250 g (8 oz) firm tofu, cubed

75 g (3 oz) dried egg thread noodles

125 g (4 oz) broccoli florets

125 g (4 oz) baby sweetcorn, halved

3 tablespoons light soy sauce

1 tablespoon lemon juice

1 teaspoon sugar

1 teaspoon chilli sauce

3 tablespoons sunflower oil

1 garlic clove, chopped

1 red chilli, deseeded and sliced

2 eggs, lightly beaten

125 g (4 oz) water chestnuts, sliced

1 Heat about 5 cm (2 inches) of vegetable oil in a wok to 180–190°C (350–375°F), or until a cube of bread browns in 30 seconds. Add the tofu and fry for 3–4 minutes, until crisp and lightly golden, then drain on kitchen paper.

2 Cook the noodles according to the packet instructions, then drain, refresh under cold water and dry well on kitchen paper. Set aside.

3 Meanwhile, blanch the broccoli and sweetcorn in a saucepan of boiling water for 1 minute, then drain, refresh under cold water and pat dry with kitchen paper. In a bowl, mix together the soy sauce, lemon juice, sugar and chilli sauce and set aside.

4 Heat the sunflower oil in a wok, add the garlic and chilli and stir-fry for 3 minutes. Add the cooked noodles and stir-fry for 5 minutes, until golden and starting to crisp up.

5 Add the eggs and stir-fry for 1 minute, then stir in the soy sauce mixture, tofu, vegetables and water chestnuts and cook for a further 2–3 minutes, until heated through. Serve immediately.

serves 4

4 crisp apples, peeled, quartered, cored and thickly sliced

sunflower oil, for deep-frying, plus 1 tablespoon

6 tablespoons sugar

2 tablespoons water

3 tablespoons golden syrup

for the batter

125 g (4 oz) plain flour

1 egg

100 ml (3½ fl oz) water

peking

toffee apples

1 In a bowl, mix together the batter ingredients, blending thoroughly to make a smooth mixture. Dip each piece of apple into the batter.

2 In a large, heavy-based saucepan or wok, heat sufficient oil for deep-frying to 180–190°C (350–375°F), or until a cube of bread browns in 30 seconds. Add the battered apple pieces and deep-fry for 2 minutes until golden. Remove with a slotted spoon and drain on kitchen paper.

3 Put the sugar, water and 1 tablespoon oil in a clean pan over a gentle heat and dissolve the sugar, stirring constantly. Add the golden syrup and boil to the hard crack stage – 151°C (304°F) on a sugar thermometer. The syrup should form brittle threads when dropped into iced water.

4 Add the fried apples to the syrup and coat all over. Remove with a slotted spoon and drop quickly into a bowl of iced water. Remove the toffee apples immediately and serve.

index

acknowledgements

Executive Editor Katy Denny
Managing Editor Clare Churly
Project Editor Alison Bolus
Contributors Susannah Blake, Georgina Charman and Cara Frost-Sharrat
Creative Director Tracy Killick
Designers Paul Reid, Lloyd Tilbury and Annika Skoog for Cobalt Id
Illustrator Annika Skoog for Cobalt id
Production Manager David Hearn